MR.★  SAM

HOW SAM WALTON BUILT WAL-MART AND BECAME AMERICA'S RICHEST MAN

KAREN BLUMENTHAL

VIKING

An Imprint of Penguin Group (USA) Inc.

VIKING
Published by Penguin Group
Penguin Group (USA) Inc., 345 Hudson Street, New York, New York 10014, U.S.A.

Penguin Books Ltd, Registered Offices: 80 Strand, London WC2R 0RL, England

First published in 2011 by Viking, a member of Penguin Group (USA) Inc.

10 9 8 7 6 5 4 3 2 1

PHOTO CREDITS: *Every effort has been made to identify the copyright holders and any omission is unintentional. We would be pleased to include the appropriate acknowledgment in any subsequent edition.* Facing p. 1: Author's collection; p. 3: Photo by Charles Bickford. Courtesy Shiloh Museum of Ozark History/*Springdale News* Collection, (SN 6-7-1985); p. 6: *Missouri Alumnus*, June 1940, University of Missouri, Columbia, M. Used with permission; p. 8: Courtesy of Flagler Productions Archives; p. 9: Courtesy of the Chisholm Trail Museum, Kingfisher, Okla.; p. 11: Reproduced from Charley Blackmore's website, www.kewpie.net; p. 17: DeGolyer Library, Southern Methodist University, Dallas, Tex., A2004.0007; p. 19: Courtesy of Unarco Industries, www.unarco.com; p. 20: DeGolyer Library, Southern Methodist University, Dallas, Tex., A2004.0007; pp. 25, 29, 30, 33: Courtesy of Flagler Productions archives; p. 40: Author's collection; p. 44: Courtesy of Flagler Productions archives; p. 47: Courtesy of Richard Berquist; p. 50: Associated Press; p. 56: Author's collection; p. 58: Courtesy of *The Dallas Morning News*; p. 61: Courtesy of the Rogers Historical Museum, Rogers, Ark. Negative #9043B; *Northwest Arkansas Times*, Sept. 29, 1964, NewspaperARCHIVE.com; p. 62: Courtesy of Flagler Productions archives; p. 67: Photo by Francis Miller, Time & Life Pictures/Getty Images; p. 71: Kresge 1962 annual report, p. 5; pp. 74, 75: Mexico, Missouri, *Ledger*, Feb. 15, 1971, NewspaperARCHIVE.com; p. 78: © Clifton Eoff, Courtesy of Flagler Productions archives. Used with permission; p. 82: Wal-Mart 1972 Annual Report, walmartstores.com; p. 84: Photos by Charles Bickford. Courtesy Shiloh Museum of Ozark History/*Springdale News* Collection, (SN 6-1972#12); p. 89: *Discount Merchandiser*, Jan. 1973, used with permission; p. 93: Photo by Jerry Biazo. Courtesy Shiloh Museum of Ozark History/*Springdale News* Collection, (SN 4-13-1972); p. 95: Fay Jones Collection (MC 1373), Special Collections, University of Arkansas Libraries, Fayetteville, Ark.; p. 100: Wal-Mart 1979 Annual Report, p. 5, walmartstores.com; p. 104: Photo by Bill Batson from the *Missouri Alumnus*, March 1978, University of Missouri, Columbia, M. Used with permission; p. 106: Newspaper-ARCHIVES.com; p. 111: Courtesy of Richard Berquist; p. 115: Courtesy of Flagler Productions archives; p. 119: Associated Press/Nancy Kaye; p. 121: Photo by Charles Bickford. Courtesy Shiloh Museum of Ozark History/*Springdale News* Collection, (SN 6-29-1984); p. 123: Courtesy of Flagler Productions archive; p. 124: Courtesy of Richard Berquist; p. 129: Wal-Mart press photo, walmartstores.com; p. 131: Photo by Marc Francoeur. Courtesy Shiloh Museum of Ozark History/*Springdale News* Collection, (SN 5-9-1990); p. 133: Associated Press/Steve McHenry; p. 139: Doonesbury © 1994 G. B. Trudeau. Reprinted by permission of Universal Uclick. All rights reserved; p. 141: Wal-Mart 1989 Annual Report, p. 6, walmartstores.com; p. 147: Photo by Deborah Billingsley; p. 151: Photo by Eli Reichman, Time & Life Images/Getty Images; p. 153: Associated Press/ J. Scott Applewhite; p. 156: Logos from the Wal-Mart website, walmartstores.com; p. 158: Wal-Mart press photo, walmartstores.com; p. 163: Both photos, Associated Press/April L. Brown; p. 165: Courtesy of John Cole

LIBRARY OF CONGRESS CATALOGING-IN-PUBLICATION DATA
Blumenthal, Karen.
Mr. Sam : how Sam Walton built Wal-Mart and became America's richest man / by Karen Blumenthal.   p. cm.
ISBN 978-0-670-01177-3 (hardcover)
1. Walton, Sam, 1918–1992—Juvenile literature. 2. Wal-Mart (Firm)—History—Juvenile literature. 3. Discount houses (Retail trade)—United States—History—Juvenile literature. 4. Businesspeople—United States—Biography—Juvenile literature. I. Title. II. Title: Mister Sam.
HC102.5.W35B47 2011   381'.149092—dc22   [B]   2010049520

Printed in U.S.A. — Set in Caslon — Book design by Kate Renner

To Ann, Kevin, and Emily,
great journalists, treasured friends

CONTENTS

This image is from a prized possession of the author's: a T-shirt from Wal-Mart's 1986 shareholders' meeting.

Introduction
Meeting Mr. Sam

THE DAY WAS young and the seats weren't yet full, but the richest man in America was already bouncing around the auditorium like a kid who had eaten too much candy. Samuel Moore Walton—Mr. Sam to many—had a microphone in his hand and was working the crowd, hustling from person to person to encourage longtime employees to share their stories about his baby, the Wal-Mart Stores chain.

As a reporter for the *Wall Street Journal*, I had been warned to arrive early on this June morning in 1986 for the 10 a.m. annual meeting of Wal-Mart's stockholders. But even 8 o'clock was barely early enough for a gathering that had started near dawn. The Wal-Mart auditorium in Bentonville, Arkansas, was filling quickly, and some people would have to watch on TV from the company cafeteria.

Mr. Sam was now sixty-eight years old, white-haired, beak-nosed, and slightly stooped, but to hundreds of Wal-Mart employees who had come to Arkansas on buses from as far as Florida, he was the closest they would ever get to American royalty. In 1962, he had opened his first Wal-Mart Discount City in nearby Rogers, Arkansas. Expanding slowly at first, and then faster and faster, the discount chain was now the nation's fifth largest retailer—and it was just getting going. Owning a big piece of it had created a Walton family fortune worth billions of dollars.

But Mr. Sam wasn't about wealth. Making gobs of money was never his goal. His passion, his love, and his laser-beam focus were, instead, *always* on his business, on rolling out new Wal-Marts and Sam's Clubs and selling mountains of underwear, socks, toys, toothpaste, and thousands of other items at lower prices than just about anyone else.

Company annual meetings are usually painfully dull, numbers-riddled affairs, but this Wal-Mart meeting was a giant pep rally, led by cheerleader Sam. In the early days, when no one in his right mind wanted to travel to Nowhere, Arkansas, Sam had a hard time getting Wall Street's attention. Then he began putting on a high-energy show for employees and other shareholders, and New York investing big shots started to attend.

Now, between the patriotic songs and slide shows, the governor of Arkansas, Bill Clinton, spoke, and two professional basketball players who had once played for the University of Arkansas came onstage to thunderous shouts and applause. Country singer Reba McEntire performed. And one executive, after promising a "pigskin" to another, actually presented him with a small, squealing pig.

Karen Blumenthal

2

Speakers rally the crowd at Wal-Mart's 1985 stockholder gathering.

Then Sam, wearing a Wal-Mart ball cap, enthusiastically pumped up the crowd.

"We've got the best group of people ever assembled in retailing!" he declared. "We're off to the best start of any Wal-Mart year in history!"

He challenged the employees in attendance to meet new and bigger goals for the next year. The crowd loudly and enthusiastically responded with the company's slogan, "Yes, we can!"

The meeting ended with Mr. Sam leading the Wal-Mart cheer: "Give me a W! Give me an A! Give me an L! Give me a squiggly"—which, properly done, was accompanied by a wiggle of the hips—and so on, until the fired up audience was roaring and ready to ring up more sales.

Afterward, Sam and his wife Helen invited the out-of-town employees to their house for box lunches, where he shook hands, posed for pictures, and visited one by one with clerks and managers from hundreds of stores.

This aw-shucks, one-of-the-guys billionaire was the public Sam Walton. The private one was more reserved, more serious, a shrewd—and sometimes ruthless—competitor who wanted nothing more than to whup the competition down the street, the stores across town, and those across the country. Money might not be that meaningful to him, but winning certainly was.

By his own admission, he relentlessly copied every good idea he could find. He would lease a building so that someone else couldn't. He raided rivals' top talent and hounded suppliers to lower their prices. He was so focused on cutting prices for customers and improving sales that he sometimes ignored other business considerations, like paying clerks well or promoting women and minorities. He shrugged off criticism that his big discount stores were destroying downtowns and demolishing local retailers in small communities. Having started as a small-town retailer himself, he saw his job as taking care of customers; other retailers could fend for themselves.

Today, about twenty-five years after that noisy, energetic meeting, Wal-Mart Stores, Inc. operates in more than fifteen countries and employs more than two million people, including well over one million in the United States. Just about two of every three Americans will shop at one of its stores, which now sport signs with a new spelling,

"Walmart," dropping the long-time hyphen to match the company's website, www.walmart.com.

Its annual sales of more than $400 billion make it the largest company in America and the largest retailer in the world, ringing up more than $1.1 billion every day, almost $800,000 every single minute.

Mr. Sam saw only glimmers of this retailing mammoth. He passed away in 1992, when Wal-Mart was one-tenth as big as it is today. Since then, its remarkable size and clout have made it increasingly controversial. Many people believe the company is too cheap in its business practices, too big, and too focused on low prices at the expense of good corporate citizenship.

But back in 1986, Sam Walton's chain was just beginning to grow out of the South and Southwest and reach toward Michigan and California. He was a regional player with an eye for great ideas, iron determination, and outrageous dreams. What he wanted most of all was to build the world's best retailer and to bring low everyday prices to every American.

By relentlessly driving for his goal, he got all that—and quite a bit more than he bargained for.

Sam Walton Is '40 Class President

Sam Moore Walton of Lexington, Mo., was elected permanent president of the Class of 1940 at class day exercises held on the campus June 3. Mr. Walton is a graduate of the College of Arts and Science and past president of QEBH senior honor society.

Miss Elizabeth Crow of Campbell, Mo., was elected vice-president, while Miss Katharine Johnson of Carrollton became secretary-treasurer by acclamation. The election of officers followed the giving of the class history by Martin Umansky, the class prophecy by Troester Goetting, and the class oration by Robert Sight.

The graduating class also elected vice-presidents for each school of the University. They are: Arts and Science, Clarence Leininger of Trenton; Agriculture, Robert Miller of Columbia; Education, Miss Ortrude Schnaebelbach of St. Louis; Business and Public Administration, Donald Hess of Crystal City; Medicine, Chester Peck of Malden; Law, James Ottman of Fairfax; Journalism, Robert Balfour of Imlay City, Mich.; Graduate, Robert Cooley of West Lafayette, Ind.; and Engineering, Dwayne Smith of Kansas City.

The taking of class pictures followed a tree planting ceremony conducted by Bob Longan of Sedalia in front of the Education Building. Near the same building, Miss Johnson, the secretary-treasurer, presided over the ivy planting. The program ended with the laying of the traditional wreath at Memorial Tower under the direction of Miss Anne Simrall of Boonville.

R.O.T.C. "Excellent"

The military department of the University received its traditional rating of "excellent" by the war department, according to word received here this month. Annual inspection was held on the campus May 9-10. In the report of the examiners, special attention was called to excellence of formations, discipline, class room conduct, courtesy, general appearance, and conduct and attitude of students out of ranks. Lieut.-Col. Lloyd E. Jones, an alumnus of the University, is commandant of the corps.

Class Day

In the top photo are shown the new officers of the Class of 1940 with President Sam Walton (front row, center) standing in front of the Education Building. (Center) Miss Katharine Johnson (left) plants the class ivy and Miss Anne Simrall (right) places the traditional class wreath in Memorial Tower. Below is the tree planting ceremony with Bob Longan presiding over the spade work. In the background is the Education Building.

Often a leader at school and in college, Sam (fourth from left in top photo) was elected president of the University of Missouri class of 1940.

Chapter 1:

Win! Win! Win!

FROM THE TIME that he was very young, Sam Walton loved to compete—and to win.

He competed—and won—in football and basketball. He ran for—and was elected to—offices in all kinds of school activities. He even managed to make the Boy Scouts competitive. When he was in grade school in Marshall, Missouri, he bet his pals that he that he would be the first one to make Eagle Scout. Before he reached his goal, though, his family moved about a hundred miles northeast, to tiny Shelbina, Missouri, a town of about 1,500 people.

Though he had to make new friends and settle into a new school, he didn't forget his boast. He kept working on his merit badges and earned his Eagle rank at the age of fifteen, which he would later say made him Shelbina's first ever Eagle Scout and the youngest person in Missouri's history at the time to earn that special rank. And, of course, he won the Eagle Scout bet with his buddies. He put his scouting skills to use when a classmate fell into a river during a picnic. Sam jumped

Sam and his younger brother, who was known as Bud.

in and pulled him out, and was credited with saving his life.

"It is a fact," he wrote later, "that I have been over-blessed with drive and ambition from the time I hit the ground."

Perhaps he was born that way. Or perhaps his rough family circumstances fired him up and convinced him that gritty determination and big goals would put him on a different life path from the difficult one his hard-working father, Tom, seemed stuck on. Thomas Gibson Walton had to deal with one lousy hand after another. He was born in 1892 in Indian Territory, later the state of Oklahoma, and both of his parents died when he was still a baby. Raised by relatives and then by a half sister in Kingfisher, Oklahoma, he came of age during some challenging years.

An uncle trained Tom to help figure out the value of farms and how to make loans on the land. In 1917, Tom married Nancy Lee Lawrence, an eighteen-year-old local farm girl. On March 29, 1918, their first child, Samuel Moore Walton, was born. Three years later, a brother, James L., known as Bud, joined him. Their mother, Nan, who was determined and driven enough to have completed a year of college before marrying, directed her own ambition toward her two boys, reading to them and making it clear that they would someday attend college.

Karen Blumenthal

The main street of Kingfisher around the time Sam was born. Walton Drug, run by an uncle of Sam's, once occupied the building on the corner.

The Waltons settled on a farm outside Kingfisher, but the years after World War I were miserable ones for farmers. Though food had been in short supply during the war, there was now a surplus. Prices fell, and many farmers struggled to make a living. Tom Walton, always a tough negotiator, tried to trade his way up, once swapping the Kingfisher farm for another one in Oklahoma. Another time, he gave up his watch in exchange for a pig that would provide meat for his family. By the time Sam was five, his parents decided it was time to give up farming and seek greener pastures in Missouri.

Tom joined a family member's mortgage company, traveling around the region to work with farmers on ways to repay loans they owed on their land, and on buying and selling farms. Sam started first grade in Springfield, Missouri, but the family moved after a few months to Marshall, a town east of Kansas City. After a few years of traveling most of each week, his dad tried to set out on his own, working in real estate and insurance. But the economy was collapsing, and the nation soon would tumble into the Great Depression.

Tom was out of work altogether before rejoining the mortgage company. This time, however, instead of helping farmers with their loans, Tom often had to take possession of farms from hundreds of owners who were deep in debt and unable to make their payments. Sam, now around twelve, sometimes went with his dad and saw the strain on the families and on his father as he tried to leave the farmers with at least some of their self-respect intact as they lost their homes and businesses. "It was tragic," Sam remembered.

To bring in some extra money, Sam's mom started a small milk business. Sam's job was to milk the cows in the morning and, after football practice, to deliver the bottles his mother prepared. To earn his own money, Sam sold magazine subscriptions door to door starting in grade school. He had jobs delivering newspapers from junior high through college, and raised and sold rabbits and young pigeons, which made a good country dinner.

He never saw himself as poor, but he knew the family was mostly scraping by at home. His school life was something altogether different. Though he wasn't a stellar student, he was a star as a student leader, and he was an intense and determined athlete.

Thanks to some experience with a grade-school football team, Sam was able to make Shelbina's varsity football team as a ninth grader. He wasn't very big—fully grown he was just five-foot-nine—but he was scrappy enough to make second-string quarterback and earn a letter. That summer, though, his parents decided to move again. Nan thought her oldest son might be a fine lawyer, and she wanted him to have a good education. So they relocated to Columbia,

The Hickman High Kewpies, led by quarterback Sam Walton (left, second from bottom), won the state championship in 1935.

home of the University of Missouri, even though that meant Tom would have to travel farther for work and Nan would take in college students as boarders to help pay the bills.

At Hickman High School, Sam really blossomed. In addition to his paper route and odd jobs, he ran track his sophomore year and became the quarterback of the football team his junior year. He wasn't fast and he didn't have a great arm, but he was the tenacious and driven leader of a team that relied more on the run than the pass. His senior year, the Kewpies went undefeated and beat their rival Jefferson City to win the state championship.

That wasn't his only amazing winning streak. Sam boasted that he never played in a losing football game. That may have been luck:

he missed some games here and there due to injuries or illness. But it also shaped his outlook.

"I have always pursued everything I was interested in with a true passion—some would say obsession—to win," he said. But that football record "taught me to expect to win, to go into tough challenges always planning to come out victorious. Later on in life, I think Kmart, or whatever competition we were facing, just became Jeff City High School."

Sam often hung out in the gym and loved playing basketball, but he didn't go out for the team, thinking he was too short. His senior year, though, he was recruited to play guard, and the basketball team went on a run as spectacular as the football team's. It also went undefeated and won the state championship.

He enjoyed leadership on and off the court, becoming class president his senior year. Not surprisingly, he was named the Most Versatile Boy in the class of 1936.

The 1936 Hickman High School *Cresset* yearbook showed Sam as a member of more than ten clubs and teams, including the library club, the speech club, the Latin club, and, for a year, the magic club. One reason he may have stayed so busy was to avoid unhappiness at home. His father was frequently on the road but when he was home, his parents fought constantly. "Mother and Dad were two of the most quarrelsome people who ever lived together," he said, and as the oldest child, he felt caught in the middle. .

Attending the University of Missouri provided another escape, and once again, he threw himself into the experience. To earn money to pay for his tuition, meals, clothes, and other expenses, he continued to deliver newspapers, waited tables in exchange for meals, and was a lifeguard. Though he was a town boy and not from the more glamorous St. Louis or Kansas City, he was accepted into a fraternity. As rush captain his sophomore year, he went all out, buying a cheap car and traveling the state to woo the best potential recruits for the fraternity even before they arrived on campus. He joined a reserve-officer military training group, attended a large Sunday School class that brought out twelve hundred students every week, and later was invited into a couple of honor societies.

Though he had girlfriends in high school, there's no record of a college sweetheart. Good-looking and athletic, "Sam did all right with the girls," a friend remembered. But between school, his many jobs, and his many activities, he didn't have much time for a social life.

In high school, he had considered a career selling insurance. A girlfriend's dad made a good living as a life insurance agent and Sam knew he could sell just about anything. But in college, he began to think his intensity and drive could to lead to something bigger. He even entertained the idea that he might one day run for president of the United States.

In the meantime, he ran for president of just about every group he participated in. His senior year, he was president of his Sunday School class, his military group, and the men's honor society. His college yearbook singled him out as one of the "Big Men on Campus."

But he also took some ribbing along with admiration from his classmates. A fraternity newsletter called him "Hustler Walton," for his eagerness to run for office, his outgoing nature, and his polished sales skills. Citing his immense energy, it called him a "heavyset hyperthyroid who sings before breakfast." As leader of the bible class, he was nicknamed "Deacon," and for his military group position, he was dubbed "Little Caesar."

As much as Sam enjoyed all his roles, the frantic pace began to wear him down. Though he was interested in going to the famous Wharton School in Pennsylvania to further his business studies, he realized that he would have to work even harder than before to pay for it. He had only briefly thought about working in retail. But now, he admitted, "I was tired and I wanted a real job."

The soon-to-be college graduate interviewed with recruiters for two companies that came through Columbia: Sears, Roebuck and Company and J. C. Penney Company. Both made him offers.

He chose Penney after an interview trip to St. Louis. "I liked what I heard," he said. "They encouraged me and thought I had the kind of talent that would be useful for them." Three days after his 1940 graduation, he was to report to Des Moines, Iowa, where he would start one of the most remarkable business careers ever.

OUR MONEY, 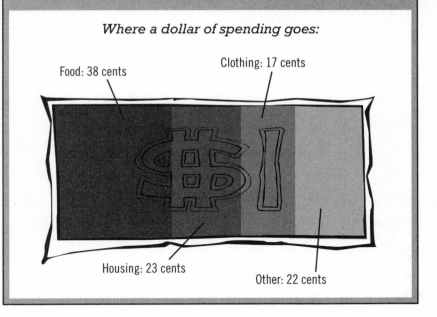 1918–19

- Average yearly income per family: $1,518 -

At the time of Sam's birth, most of a typical family's spending goes toward paying for basic needs. Below is a breakdown of what percentage of an average family's budget goes to food, housing, and other essentials and what is left over for extras like entertainment—in other words, where the average dollar goes.

Where a dollar of spending goes:

Food: 38 cents

Clothing: 17 cents

Housing: 23 cents

Other: 22 cents

Mr. Sam

Chapter 2:

War!

SAM DIDN'T KNOW much about retailing or J. C. Penney when he was hired for $75 a month plus commissions. He didn't know that he would end up following in the footsteps of the renowned James Cash Penney. But he did know that he wanted to do well for his demanding manager, Duncan Major.

Early on, the trainees were introduced to Penney's core principles: The company should satisfy the public and seek fair—but not excessive—profits from sales. It would reward managers and associates, the term Penney used for its employees. It would offer customers value and quality for their dollar. And it would expect associates to ask of every policy and act, "Does it square with what is right and just?"

In case Sam wasn't convinced that the company was serious, his boss helped remind him—especially when Major received a bonus check for thousands of dollars, representing his share of the store's profits. That amount left a significant impression on a young man whose salary was less than $1,000 a year.

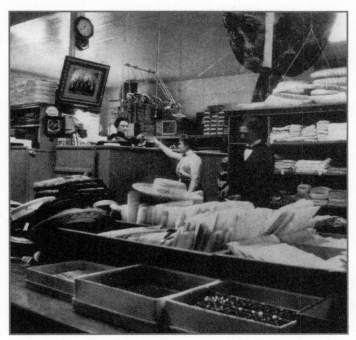

James Cash Penney tends to a Golden Rule store in Wyoming, circa 1906.

Major steeped his trainees in Penney's culture, requiring them to come in at 6:30 in the morning and working them until 7 or 8 every evening, Monday through Saturday. On Sundays, he invited the young men to his house to play ping-pong or cards and to talk shop and share retailing ideas. "It was a seven-day job," Sam recalled.

The company that would put Sam through basic training was born in the early part of the twentieth century, as American factories were beginning to churn out shirts, suits, dresses, shoes, gloves, stockings, silverware, lamps, dishes, rugs, jewelry, and even pianos that could be delivered to stores via an expanding network of rail lines. With more goods available, fancy department stores sprang up in cities, featuring silk gowns, lace, and the latest fashions, as well as rugs and books, with dozens of departments catering to those with money to spend. New York had several, including the elegant Macy's and Bloomingdale's, Chicago had a sprawling Marshall Field's store, Philadelphia had Wannamaker's, and Boston, Filene's.

Two other companies, Sears, Roebuck and Company, and Montgomery Ward, sent huge catalogs full of useful products, from clothing to sewing machines to farm equipment, to people outside of cities, charging prices that were far less than local merchants'. (These catalogs were useful in other ways: They were often placed in the outhouse where the pages provided fascinating reading material and sometimes served other duties.) Shoppers looking for a bargain just had to have the patience to wait for an item to be delivered by mail.

Penney started in small towns with one-room general stores, which grew into small department stores filled with reasonably priced work clothes, underwear, shoes, fabrics, and sewing materials. The chain opened its five hundredth store in 1924, and by the end of the 1920s, it had more than one thousand outlets, largely in the Midwest and the West. By then, its customers had moved from using their nickels and dimes to buy basic necessities to wanting more and more of all kinds of things: fashionable clothes, perfumes and creams, time-saving appliances like refrigerators, toasters, and vacuum cleaners, and entertainment like phonographs, radios, and even exotic pets.

During this time, as an increasing number of people moved to cities and cars grew common, chains of all kinds grew at a brisk pace. There were chains of movie theaters, grocery chains, drugstore

HOW SYLVAN GOLDMAN MOVED THE WORLD

While stores like J. C. Penney had clerks in every department to help customers, supermarkets were moving toward "self-service," allowing customers to make their own selections from the shelves.

But carrying all their groceries around the store was a problem for shoppers, since baskets with groceries in them were heavy to carry. In the mid-1930s, Sylvan N. Goldman, president of the Standard-Humpty Dumpty Super Markets of Oklahoma City, Oklahoma, began tinkering with a folding chair.

By adding wheels, he could push the chair around, and by adding a basket to the seat, he created a moving cart. Even better, he realized, if he raised the seat a few inches, he could put a second basket underneath.

He hurried to a store on a Saturday for the basket carrier's big debut. But to his shock, he said, "it was a complete flop." Women waved it off, saying, "I have been pushing enough baby carriages." Men turned it down, too, saying they were strong enough to carry their own baskets.

Finally, he hired men and women of different ages to push merchandise-filled carts around the store. Only then did the buggies take off.

In 1937, Goldman formed the Folding Carrier Basket Company, now Unarco, which became the world's largest shopping-cart maker. Over time, baskets were made bigger and the carts were made to nest together for storage. Realizing that mothers often shopped with their children, designers in 1947 added a child's seat in front—and then, in 1952, they added a plastic flap for shoppers without children to close up the leg holes.

chains, and the beginnings of hotel and restaurant chains. Their size helped them negotiate better deals with suppliers, allowing them to offer lower prices. During the Great Depression, however, when small businesses were especially hard hit, there was a major political move to stall the growth of chains to protect local mom-and-pop groceries and general stores. But few of the efforts stuck, and the end result was that chains opened bigger stores than ever.

By the time Sam arrived at Penney, two other chains, Sears, Roebuck and Montgomery Ward, also had hundreds of stores. Always

The J. C. Penney store in Des Moines, where Sam worked, was across the street from Sears.

competitive, Sam frequently wandered across the street to study the Des Moines Sears store during his lunch hour. Other times, to get a leg up on another trainee, he would shorten his lunch break to fifteen minutes so that he could make more sales.

Though Sam seemed like a promising recruit, not everyone was supportive of him. A man from headquarters named Blake frequently came to the Des Moines store to keep tabs on how associates were doing. He admired young Walton's sales skills but was frustrated by the trainee's shoddy handling of sales slips, his messy handwriting, and his willingness to leave paperwork unfinished if a customer was waiting. In the days well before computers, such disregard for record-keeping made it hard to keep good track of sales.

"Maybe you're just not cut out for retail," Blake told him one day.

But Sam felt at home on the sales floor, and he remembered, "I loved retail from the very beginning." He liked his new job so much that he convinced his brother Bud, a recent military school graduate, to join Penney, too, starting in Cedar Rapids, Iowa.

One day, James Cash Penney himself came into the store and watched young Sam wrap up a package. After the customer left, Penney called Sam and another salesman over, saying, "I want to show you something."

Deftly, the retailing legend took a similar sized box and wrapped it with paper that overlapped by barely a quarter of an inch, tying it all on with just a bit of string. Always the frugal merchant, Penney told his young colleagues, tongue in cheek, "Boys, you know we don't make a dime out of the merchandise we sell. We only make our profit

PENNEY PINCHING

In many ways, James Cash Penney, the founder of the J. C. Penney stores, traveled a path similar to the young hire who joined his Des Moines store in 1940.

Born in 1875 on a farm near Hamilton, Missouri, Jim Penney, too, grew up in rural Missouri in a family where money was often tight. Like Sam, Penney started his business education early. When he was eight, his father informed him, "From now on you'll be buying your own clothes." The youngster tried to bargain. His shoes had holes in them. Could he get one more pair first?

His father wouldn't budge.

After high school, Penney couldn't afford college. Realizing he was lousy at farming, he began working in a local store called Golden Rule. He enjoyed the work, and when he moved to Denver, Colorado, for health reasons, he landed a job at a store run by two partners. By 1902, they were so impressed with the twenty-seven-year-old that they asked him to open a store in Wyoming and made him a part owner. A few years later, he would buy out their interest in three stores and begin expanding, eventually putting the Penney name on the doors.

It was in his first store that Penney learned one of his most enduring lessons. His customers paid with pennies, nickels, and dimes, not dollars, and since every penny counted to them, every cent mattered to the man Penney as well. "We threw away no wrapping paper, no short ends of string, no empty boxes, no nails, even though they were bent, for they could be straightened and used again," he said. That frugality was part of the company's culture for many years—and it would also become a trademark of Sam Walton.

out of the paper and string we save!" Sam got the message that every penny counts.

Though Sam enjoyed the work, he also realized that he might be drafted into the army soon. With much of Europe already at war in 1941, Americans were on edge, knowing that they could be pulled into the conflict at any time. Already, some merchandise was growing scarce. The Penney company newsletter warned in September 1941 that the supply of silk stockings would run out within sixty days, with all available silk going to the war effort. Nylon stocking replacements, the company said, wouldn't be available for several months.

The bombing of Pearl Harbor in December 1941 brought America into World War II. Knowing that he would be drafted soon, Sam quit his Penney position in early 1942, after just about a year and a half in Des Moines, and headed to Oklahoma to work temporarily while he waited for his military assignment. Sam ended up in Claremore, Oklahoma, taking a job at a nearby gunpowder plant.

Even with the war raging, Sam's sudden departure was uncharacteristic and it apparently was prompted by something else. Against Penney rules, which banned romances among employees, Sam had been dating a cashier at the store. She was interested in marrying him. He didn't share her enthusiasm, and leaving Des Moines was a quick way out. But it was only after she visited Oklahoma that he truly broke off the relationship.

He clearly didn't spend a lot of time moping about it. That April, Sam met Helen Robson at a Claremore bowling alley. She had just taken her turn and was coming back to sit down when Sam, leg hanging over a chair armrest, dropped one of the world's oldest opening lines. "Haven't I met you somewhere before?" he asked her.

Turned out, he had. Helen, the valedictorian of her high school class in Claremore, had attended Christian College for Women in Columbia, Missouri, at the same time that Sam had been at the bigger University of Missouri. He had dated a girl she knew, and once had refereed a swim meet in which Helen had competed. After two years in Missouri, Helen had gone on to earn a bachelor of science degree in business at the University of Oklahoma, with a minor in secretarial science—the minor encouraged by her father, who wanted her to have useful skills right out of school.

Helen had toyed with the idea of law school, but her father, a lawyer who had become a successful banker and rancher, urged her to stay home for a year, with the promise of helping her achieve whatever she wanted after that. She ended up working in his office and keeping the books for him, while also taking flying lessons to learn to pilot a small airplane. "I wanted to fly so bad I just couldn't stand it," she said. She advanced to flying solo and had logged three or four hours alone in the air before her wings were clipped. She was grounded so that men could be trained for the military.

Sam was smitten. He found Helen pretty and smart, energetic and athletic, and opinionated and strong-willed enough to hold her own. He also grew very fond of her father, Leland Stanford Robson, one of the most prosperous men in the region. Robson would light Sam's passion for quail hunting and become Sam's guide and mentor in building a business.

Sam and Helen were married on Valentine's Day, while he was on a short leave from military service.

Helen had other suitors, but she saw in Sam a kind of energy and drive that she believed would make him successful. "I thought life with him would be interesting," she said later.

Sam was called into the military just a couple of months later. Because of a mild heart irregularity discovered during his army physical, he could serve stateside, and not in combat. By the time he left for service in the West, however, he knew he had found two loves: the woman he wanted to marry and the career he wanted in retail.

Sam Walton and Helen Alice Robson were married on Valentine's Day, 1943, in a candlelight ceremony that was the talk of Claremore. She wore a simple but elegant dress with a square neckline and long, wide train. Sam, on a three-day pass from the army, wore his military dress uniform. His brother Bud, a navy pilot, flew in to be the best man. After the wedding, Helen flew back to California with Sam.

During his time in the military, he supervised security at aircraft plants and prisoner-of-war camps.

Helen returned to Claremore in the fall of 1944 to give birth to their first child, Samuel Robson Walton, whom they called Rob. In August 1945, Sam was discharged and ready to embark on a retail adventure.

Initially, he wanted to settle in St. Louis, Missouri, and start a small department store with an old buddy. But Helen, who had moved sixteen times with Sam in their first two years of marriage, now had a say in the matter, and her request was straightforward: She didn't want to live in any town with more than ten thousand people. And she didn't want Sam to start out in a business partnership, because she believed they often didn't work out. Sam listened.

Sam and his friend had been considering working with Butler Brothers, a company that sold wholesale goods and helped businessmen set up their own department stores. Butler also had a small-town chain of Ben Franklin variety stores, which carried an oddball mix of inexpensive items ranging from small toys and penny candy to sewing accessories, cooking utensils, and toothpaste. As luck would have it, a Ben Franklin store in Newport, Arkansas, a cotton and railroad town with a population of five or six thousand, was for sale. Twenty-seven-year-old Sam Walton was about to become a real merchant.

OUR MONEY, 1945

- Average yearly family income: $2,621 -

As World War II draws to an end, American families begin to regroup and think about buying cars, houses, and new appliances. The government didn't survey actual spending during the decade, so their exact spending isn't known.

Number of family households: 34.5 million

Households in rural areas, but not on farms: 21%   Households on farms: 17%   Households in urban areas: 62%

Chapter 3:

Sell! Sell! Sell!

THE BEN FRANKLIN store in Newport turned out to be, in Sam's own words, "a real dog."

Still in his army uniform, Sam had ridden the train from Missouri to northeast Arkansas to clinch the deal, paying $25,000—$5,000 of his own savings and $20,000 borrowed from Helen's father. But he hadn't done all his homework. The rent turned out to be unusually high, and Sterling, a competing variety store across the street, was doing twice as much business.

He spent two weeks at the Ben Franklin store in Arkadelphia, Arkansas, to learn the ropes, and took over his new store on September 1, 1945. Butler Brothers made it easy for a fellow who was better at selling and scheming than at handling paperwork. It provided manuals for keeping track of inventory and sales, figuring out profits and losses, and comparing today's business to the same day last year. The forms were so straightforward and simple that Sam would use Butler Brothers' methods for the next two decades.

But since Butler Brothers made its money by buying huge quantities of goods from manufacturers and then selling them at a higher price to its store owners, it also wanted to dictate most of what Sam put on the shelves and the prices he paid for the merchandise. Sam soon realized that if he could buy at least some of his merchandise cheaper, he could sell it for less, and that would give him an edge against the other stores in town.

Sam set out on his own to find better deals for his store. Variety stores, as their name implied, carried a huge range of goods. The first variety store, started by Frank W. Woolworth back in 1879, sold nothing for more than five cents. The next year, he added a ten-cent line. The Woolworth stores became known as "five-and-tens" or "five-and-dimes" and sold almost anything that could be bought for a dime or less.

Sam's first store, in Newport, Arkansas.

Sam and Bud as young men, probably in the early 1940s.

By the time Sam Walton came along, variety-store prices were much higher, but most items were still cheap compared with department stores or local dress shops. The candy aisle of a variety store was usually the best in town, with both candy bars and penny candy, sold individually or by the ounce. The toy department was a child's dream, with counters full of metal action figures, doll clothes, yo-yos, paints, trucks, checkers, comic books, and coloring books. One aisle might have pens, pencils, and other office supplies, another would have dishes, crockery, and drinking glasses, and a couple more would stock toothpaste, shampoo, and aspirin. The biggest section, though, was for everyday clothing.

Dresses, suits, and fancy hats were sold at stores like J. C. Penney, which had an outlet next door to Sam's Ben Franklin. The variety stores had inexpensive baby clothes and children's wear, purses and hosiery, shirts, and underwear for all.

Eager to build his business, Sam worked in the Ben Franklin store during the day and then took off at closing for a distributor in Tennessee, with a trailer hitched to his car. There he would load up on good deals for shirts and socks. "I'd bring them back, price them low, and just blow the stuff out of the store," he said.

Before long, he found an even cheaper supplier in New York and learned one of his most important business lessons: Lower prices could mean higher sales and profits.

Sam was paying Butler Brothers $2.50 a dozen for ladies' satin, elastic-waist panties and was selling them for three for $1. That meant each dozen was bringing in $4 in sales and $1.50 in profit.

But Weiner Buying Services in New York was willing to sell Sam the same undies for $2 a dozen. Sam tagged them at four for $1 and they flew off the shelves. At that bargain price, he was bringing in sales of $3 for each dozen and $1 in profit—but he sold so many more panties that his total sales and profits were higher. "This is really the essence of discounting," he said later. But the enormous potential for him to pull off his panty experience on a national scale wouldn't become apparent for many more years.

In addition to trying to build his business, he had other distractions. Sam had jumped into civic affairs with the same zeal he had shown in joining high school and college clubs. He was a member of the Rotary Club and a deacon at his Presbyterian church, and served on the town's board of public affairs and as president of the Chamber of Commerce, which supported local businesses.

As was common in family businesses, Sam got support and advice from Helen, but she was also busy with a growing family. John Thomas was born in October 1946, not quite two years after Rob. James Carr, or Jim, followed in June 1948, and the only daughter, Alice, arrived in October 1949. With four children in five years, Helen had her hands full—and her husband was often working or busy with other things. "I became accustomed to putting the babies to bed at night alone," she said. "I always read to the children, and we read a lot of good books that way. They never went to bed without a story."

In Newport, Sam began to hone habits that would define his business style. Always careful with his pennies in his personal life, he was just as cheap as a store owner. Rather than hire more help, he and his brother, Bud, who had moved with his wife, Audie, to Newport after the war, did everything: sweeping the floors, washing the windows, checking in the stock, and designing the store displays. "We had to keep expenses to a minimum," Bud said. "Our money was made by controlling expenses."

Just as he had regularly scoured the Sears store across from J. C. Penney in Des Moines, Sam was frequently in the Sterling store across the street, studying prices, products, and displays. He became fascinated with merchandise displays and studied how to best pack in and promote his goods. And he broiled over the fact that a store that was a little smaller than his could do so much more business.

Sam was friendly with the Sterling manager, joining him

occasionally for coffee, but he was also determined to win. The Sterling store was the first in town to stock women's rayon underwear, with the fancy pants selling for a pricey 39 cents. When the store's entire stock sold out in a single day, Sam took note.

Wanting a piece of the action, Sam rushed to Little Rock to buy up everything that Sterling's supplier had available—before Sterling could reorder.

By Sam's third year, he had more than doubled his Ben Franklin store's sales to $175,000 from $72,000 in the year before he bought it. He had repaid his loan to Helen's father. And he was finally catching up to the Sterling store.

Through the town grapevine, he learned that the Sterling

The growing Walton family, Sam, Jim, Rob, John, Helen, and baby Alice, in 1950.

manager planned to take over a small Kroger grocery next door and expand his store. Sam couldn't bear the thought—especially because he might never be able to catch up. So he sought out the landlady in Hot Springs, 140 miles away, and grabbed the lease before Sterling could get to it.

He named the new store Eagle—"that's all I could think of"—without any idea what he would put in it. He called it a department store and sold a bit more clothing in it than in his Ben Franklin store, though observers said there wasn't much difference in the two outlets. When items weren't selling in one store, he ran them down the alley in hopes of selling them in the other. While his Ben Franklin business grew, however, the Eagle store was pretty much a dud.

But since he had blocked Sterling's expansion, he didn't really care. "I figured I'd rather have a small profit than have my competitor over there in a big store," he said. Sam managed to stay on good terms with the Sterling manager, and years later, after the manager retired, he laughed about Sam's competitiveness. But, said Helen, at the time, "I'm sure it aggravated him quite a bit."

While experimenting with Eagle, Sam also kept tinkering with ways to improve his Ben Franklin. To draw customers, he put a popcorn machine on the sidewalk, and the aroma drew in shoppers like metal to a magnet. Seeing the crowds, he added a soft-serve ice cream machine, which proved just as popular—except with his brother Bud.

Bud hated milk—always had—and as a kid, Sam used to torment his little brother when he milked the cow by squirting milk at him. Now

Sam assigned the important job of cleaning the ice cream machine to Bud. (Perhaps not surprisingly, Bud and Audie moved to Versailles, Missouri, to run their own Ben Franklin store not too long after.) Though Bud and Sam would work together for most of their lives, "I never forgave him for making me clean out that damned ice cream machine," Bud said. But years later, Sam still thought it was funny.

RETAIL DETAIL

Wholesale, Retail, and Markups

In addition to paying for merchandise and sales help, retailers also must pay for rent, electricity, headquarters' offices, salaries, taxes, and other costs.

To do that, retailers buy goods from manufacturers at a "wholesale" price, or the maker's price, and sell the merchandise at a "retail" price to customers. The difference, sometimes called the "markup," provides the money and profit needed to run a business.

When Sam was starting out, most retailers marked up goods from 50 percent to 100 percent, selling, say, an item purchased for $2 wholesale for $3 or $4 retail. But Sam might sell that $2 item for only $2.50 or $2.75.

Sam got another good laugh when a J. C. Penney official named Blake came to town to audit the neighboring Penney store—the same Blake who once thought young Sam Walton should find another line of work. The manager of the Newport Penney told Blake about the ex-Penney man who had a booming Ben Franklin outlet and a second store.

Blake didn't believe him. "It can't be the same one," he said. "That fellow couldn't have amounted to anything." He was shocked to find the same Sam Walton next door.

Blake may have been wrong about Sam's future, but he was

absolutely correct about his sloppiness with details and paperwork. By now, the little Ben Franklin was bringing in sales of $250,000 a year, making profits of $30,000 to $40,000, and ranking as the chain's top performer in the whole six-state region. But Sam's five-year lease would be up within the year and when he went to negotiate a renewal, he discovered his landlord had the upper hand. In his rush to become a real merchant, Sam had neglected to be sure his lease included an option that allowed him to easily renew it.

His landlord, impressed with Sam's success, wanted his own son to run the store. The landlord refused to renew the lease at any price—though he did offer a fair price for the store and the merchandise, and he honored the lease until the end of 1950, giving Sam time to figure out what to do.

Sam was devastated. He was upset with himself, furious with the landlord, and in hot water with Helen, who didn't want to move with four young children. That setback was compounded by a tragedy that fall, when his mother Nan needed surgery for cancer. He and Bud hurried to St. Louis, but sadly she died soon after, on September 29, at the age of fifty-two.

Sam dealt with the losses as best he could. While the Ben Franklin store went to the landlord, he sold his lease on the Eagle store to the Sterling folks so that his competitor could expand and maybe challenge the new owners. He also began to encourage six-year-old Rob to become a lawyer someday.

"It really was like a nightmare," Sam said. "I had built the best variety store in the whole region and worked hard in the community—done everything right—and now I was being kicked out of town. It didn't seem fair."

But there was nothing he could do about it. He and Helen would have to start over.

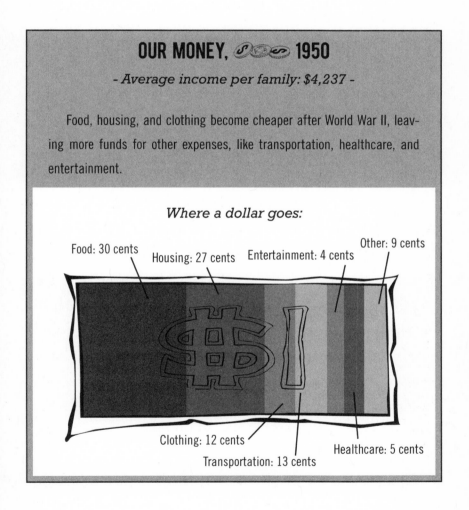

OUR MONEY, 1950

- Average income per family: $4,237 -

Food, housing, and clothing become cheaper after World War II, leaving more funds for other expenses, like transportation, healthcare, and entertainment.

Where a dollar goes:

Food: 30 cents

Housing: 27 cents

Entertainment: 4 cents

Other: 9 cents

Clothing: 12 cents

Transportation: 13 cents

Healthcare: 5 cents

Chapter 4:

Flying!

IN SEARCH OF a new store, Sam and Helen drove through the small towns of northwest Arkansas, an area that was near Claremore and Helen's parents. One of their trips took them to Bentonville, Arkansas, a little blip of a town in the far northwest corner of the state, with just three thousand people, half the size of Newport. In the scenic area known as the Ozarks, Bentonville was more than one hundred miles from Tulsa, Oklahoma, and even farther from Little Rock or Kansas City, Missouri. But the owner of the Harrison's variety store on the town square was nearing retirement. And maybe more notably, this was a town in need of some well-priced panties.

There was another attraction: Thanks to Helen's father, Sam had become an avid quail hunter, and Bentonville was near the border of four states—Arkansas, Missouri, Kansas, and Oklahoma—so Sam could make the most of four slightly different winter hunting seasons.

To ensure that Helen and Sam would never face eviction again, Helen's father personally negotiated to buy the store's building from the out-of-state landlords. To expand the tiny store, Sam also took over the barbershop next door—with a ninety-nine year lease.

In May 1950, the local newspaper declared that a "big business deal" had been completed and crowed with unusual foresight about the new arrivals: "It is a big accomplishment to have people such as the Waltons come here to live, as this is a fine family and their progressive plans mean much to the business life of this city." At thirty-two years old, Sam merely planned to expand the original store—but his "progressive plans" would take on far greater meaning in future years.

Sam took over the Bentonville store while his Newport days were still winding down. He tore out the wall between the original store and the barbershop to create 4,000 square feet, a space smaller than the Newport store. He renamed the store Walton's 5 & 10, and that summer he held a huge remodeling sale, filling big barrels with sale items, like ten dishcloths for 39 cents, (regularly two for 15 cents); "lovely" girls' dresses for $1.29, down from $1.98; Cannon bath towels for 29 cents; and ladies' panties, an "exceptional value" at 29 cents.

More memorable than the special bargain prices, however, were the women who came in and bent way over to reach into the barrels, unintentionally flashing their unmentionables. Sam watched them, frowning, and realized he had a challenge. "One thing we gotta do," he told Charlie Baum, an early employee. "We gotta be real strong in lingerie."

Sam called his Bentonville store Walton's; today, the store is the Wal-Mart Visitor Center, which celebrates the company's history.

"Times had been hard," Baum recalled, "and some of those underthings were pretty ragged."

The sale was followed by more remodeling, and in early March 1951, Sam closed the store for a week or so to prepare for a grand reopening. New tables and racks had been built, new fluorescent lights brightened the space, and completely new merchandise was brought in. Still, the store was lacking: It didn't have a back door. Upstairs, a tiny attic room served as an office. Sam put a plank between two sawhorses to make a desk, and he nailed a crate to the wall to hold his books. For the next several years, this would be his executive suite.

Bad weather delayed the renovation of the outside, but the newspaper promised it would be "an attractive addition to the Bentonville shopping district when complete."

To bring in old and new customers, the grand reopening offered two full newspaper pages of specials on a wide range of items, such as 15-cent baby bottles, 27-cent floor wax, 29-cent work socks, an 8-cent box of Crayola crayons, a bottle of Wonder Bubbles with a wand for 9 cents, 98-cent men's ties, and at least three kinds of women's panties. Shoppers who were in the store when an alarm clock rang would get a free goldfish, though the container for it cost 3 cents. Another full page of ads came from local lumber and paint companies and even the local bank, congratulating the "up and coming businessman" on his new store.

Despite its exciting specials, the new Walton's 5 & 10 was an old-fashioned store. Every department had clerks to help customers select items, ring up sales, and wrap the purchases. The pricing was old-fashioned, too. If Sam got a great deal on, say, socks or paper towels, he could offer a special price; he also could offer special prices on brand names for a few days. But for the most part, a brand-name manufacturer could insist that Sam sell at the manufacturer's recommended price under "fair trade" laws enacted around 1930. State and federal lawmakers had pushed through the laws at the beginning of the Great Depression to protect small, local retailers like Sam Walton. They worried that big chains like J. C. Penney, Sears, and

Montgomery Ward got much better prices on goods by buying in huge quantities and they would use that pricing power to bully the little guys out of business.

As a result, the competing variety stores in a town might carry many of the same items at roughly the same prices. So only a few things set one store apart from another: Were the clerks helpful and friendly? Was the store clean? And perhaps most important, would the items people needed be available? Stores that always had a good supply of basics on the shelves, like black or white thread, zippers, or cotton socks, would be more successful than those that were frequently out of stock.

Sam's store, despite the Walton name, was still a Ben Franklin franchise, and most of what he sold had to come from the Ben Franklin folks at prices they set. But he wanted to improve on that, and wherever he could, he would. His little store had brought in just $32,000 in sales the year before he bought it. This grew to about $90,000 the first year he owned it; still, that was less than half the sales he had rung up in Newport.

Perhaps recognizing that Bentonville was only going to be able to offer so much business, he began looking around for a second location and discovered that Kroger was leaving a long skinny space in the town square in Fayetteville, about thirty miles to the south. Jumping into a new trend in retailing, this would be Sam's first "self service" store, without clerks at each counter and with all the cash registers up front.

Knowing he couldn't run two stores by himself, Sam began what would be a long tradition: raiding competitors for talent. He met Willard Walker while visiting a TG&Y store in Tulsa that Walker was managing and quizzed him for about an hour. Not long after, Sam asked Walker to be his Fayetteville manager. Money was so tight that Walker would have to move himself and work for free until the store opened. Walker gambled that getting a salary and a percentage of the store's profits would be a lucrative move for his family.

As he had in Newport and in college, Sam jumped into civic affairs, joining the Rotary Club and serving on the Chamber of Commerce board. For years, he joined other businessmen early in the morning for coffee at a local café, chitchatting about business, politics, and sports. He stayed in shape and kept his competitive edge by playing tennis, often spending his lunch hour on the court.

Sam consulted Helen about business matters, and she helped interview new managers and their wives, since working for the small company was something of a family affair. But Helen was more visible in the community and at the Presbyterian Church, while Sam was most often seen at his stores. Still, when their boys got older, he served as a scoutmaster, and he even taught Sunday School for a while—though Helen typically had to get the four kids up and ready for church by herself.

While he would work even longer hours later on, Helen said,

The Walton family circa late 1950s: Alice, John, Rob, and Jim with Sam and Helen.

"Don't get the idea he wasn't working most of the time before that." Some weekday nights, he still drove to Tennessee to stuff his station wagon with merchandise for his stores, and since Saturday was a big day for sales, Sam worked all day Saturday and usually Saturday night.

While the children were growing up, he was still a small-town merchant, and most years, the family took a month off each summer for a camping vacation. They'd fill the station wagon with the kids and the dog, tie a canoe on top, hitch a trailer on the back, and head for the Carolinas or the Grand Canyon or Yellowstone National Park. Even on vacation, his son Jim said, "Dad thrived on change" and would quickly rearrange plans, especially if an interesting store was nearby. No matter where they went, Sam had to stop and look at other stores, comparing layouts, prices, and merchandise to his own.

As the boys moved into high school in the late 1950s and early 1960s, Sam made an effort to be at their Friday night football games. On weekends when Alice was in junior high and high school, Sam often took her to quarter-horse shows. Helen thought he stayed to watch. But Alice remembers, "Dad and I had a pact: He would drop me off, and I would show my horses, while he would go look at stores."

Years later, in a visit with local elementary school students, Sam was asked if his children suffered from his frequent travel. "I probably could have done more with them and maybe trained them better," he answered. "My wife had most of the responsibility. That's one of the prices you pay."

All four children were expected to work in the stores, sweeping floors, carrying boxes, stocking shelves, or doing whatever else had to be done. The boys also had paper routes and chores around the house, like mowing the lawn. Starting as a little girl, Alice helped with the candy counter or popcorn machine, and when she got older, she sometimes went with her dad to visit stores.

Though Sam expected them to work hard, he wasn't as demanding as Helen in some ways. Helen, the former valedictorian, wasn't satisfied with Bs on her kids' report cards, pushing them by saying, "I made all As and I know you can do it," Alice remembered. Her dad, by contrast, would say, "This is what I made. As and Bs are pretty good."

From the time they were young, the Walton kids were also owners in the stores. Helen's father, Leland S. Robson, told Sam that he had made his children partners in his real-estate and banking business nearly from the beginning, and he coached Sam to do the same thing. One reason was to involve the kids in the business early so they would understand it when they grew up. By making them partners, the family also ensured that control would pass from one generation to another. A third reason was to avoid inheritance taxes later. If the children shared the ownership when the business wasn't worth much, they wouldn't have to worry about paying inheritance taxes down the road, when it might be worth a lot more. So in 1953, Sam's and Helen's stake in the two stores became part of a partnership in which the couple owned 20 percent and each of their four young children owned 20 percent; from then on, almost everything they owned would be shared with their kids.

The family business was a major topic of dinner conversation. The young Waltons were encouraged to save, and, as the company grew, even to invest their savings in their father's new stores to become bigger owners. Years later, John Walton estimated that the small investments in individual stores that he made with savings from his paper route and his time in the army had grown along with the company, reaching about $40 million by the early 1990s.

None of the family expected anything like that back in the 1950s,

Sam's first office above the store (recreated at the Wal-Mart Visitor Center) was small and spare.

when new stores were expensive to open, since the lease, improvements, and merchandise had to be paid for before the first sale was recorded. Though Helen had a fair bit of family wealth, she was as careful with her pennies as Sam was.

Monte Harris grew up near the Walton store in Bentonville, and her mother took in sewing jobs. Helen would bring in the children's jeans for patching, over and over and over again. Finally, the seamstress pointed out that there had to be something left of the pants in order for them to be patched. "This was a very frugal woman," Harris remembered.

Though Sam was conservative with a buck at home, he was

SAM STORIES: THE MISTAKE

Part of building a strong and successful business is cultivating myths and legends that become rooted in the company's culture. These stories, some of which may be embellished, illustrate a company's values and help bind employees together with a common goal.

Over the years, Sam would earn a reputation for being willing to recognize his mistakes and cut his losses when an idea wasn't working. He often said he learned that lesson from his biggest mistake.

After he was bowled over by the Kansas City shopping center in the early 1950s, he was certain that such shopping centers were "going to sweep the country."

"I was going to be a shopping center magnate," he said. "I thought it was a pure cinch."

He leased forty acres in Little Rock and convinced a Kroger and a Woolworth store to rent space. He made up brochures by hand and went door-to-door collecting signatures on a petition to get a road paved. But progress on the center was slow, and after two years, he had invested all the money he wanted to put into it.

"I decided I had better take my whipping," he said. He lost about $25,000 at a time when he and Helen "were counting every dollar." The hopeful shopping center tycoon turned his attention back to retailing.

Sam's instincts were right—he was just too early. Shopping centers did sweep the country, and the spot he tried to develop became a very successful center a few years later.

willing to spend to expand the business. In 1954, he and Bud joined together to open a Ben Franklin in a brand-spanking-new shopping center near a new housing development in Kansas City. Right away, they realized the promise of these shopping centers and their vast parking lots that were springing up several miles away from the downtown stores. The new store brought in $250,000 in sales the first year, more than Sam's other two stores combined, and sales kept growing.

Sam wanted to expand further, but he was frustrated by the hours he spent navigating the country roads between his stores. One day, he called his brother, the former navy pilot, and asked him to come to Kansas City to help him buy a plane.

Bud flat out refused. Sam was "the world's worst driver," easily distracted and always in a hurry. "I figured anyone who drove a car like Sam sure didn't need to be in an airplane," Bud said. He tried to talk his big brother out of it, but Sam had made up his mind. Eventually, Sam bought a rattly used plane. "It had a washing machine motor in it, and it would putt-putt, and then miss a lick, then putt-putt again," Bud said. The radio was so bad "it would have been just as effective to open the cockpit door and use a megaphone to communicate." Bud refused to fly in the plane for more than a year.

Sam, raring to go, ignored his brother, hired an instructor, and learned to fly. And once he could get to and from stores easily, his business took off as well. Sam added variety stores in Little Rock, Siloam Springs, and Springdale, Arkansas, and two more in Kansas.

Sam was always in need of start-up money, so each store had a different combination of owners. Bud nearly always invested. Sometimes their father, Tom Walton, joined them, as did Helen's father and her two brothers, store managers, and occasionally the Walton kids.

Though Sam was building a good-sized chain for an independent businessman, it was still a low-budget operation, run by a couple of brothers and managers, partly out of the back of a station wagon. Sam picked up merchandise on a whim, and often had a good eye for hot trends. Once, on a buying trip to New York, he came back with a binful of a new shoe, a "zori" sandal, that was little more than a thin rubber platform and a y-shaped strap that fit between the first and

Hula hoops were the hot toy in the late 1950s.

second toes. His sales clerks were sure they would just leave custom-ers with blisters.

But he tied them together and priced them at 19 cents a pair. The shoes—what we later called thongs and now call flip-flops—galloped out of the store, until nearly everyone in Bentonville had a pair.

In the later 1950s, when hula hoops were the hottest toy around, little stores had a hard time getting a supply, and they were expensive, besides. Sam convinced another Ben Franklin owner to team up with him to make their own. They bought miles of small plastic pipe in four-teen colors and set up an assembly line, cutting nine-foot lengths and connecting the ends with a plug and a staple. They made thousands of them. Sam packed his share in a makeshift trailer attached to his car and delivered them to stores, where they sold like crazy for a dollar each.

In the early 1960s, Sam spotted St. Robert, Missouri,

from the air, a nothing little burg on the edge of a huge military base that was in need of a real retail store to compete with the army com-missary. Gary Reinboth was managing a variety store in Omaha, Nebraska, and barely making enough to support his family of four, when he inquired about a position with Ben Franklin. Sam Walton heard about him and called to ask if he'd be interested in managing a new store. Reinboth couldn't afford to take time off or travel for an interview, so Bud flew up to meet him, wearing old khakis and cowboy boots.

Bud interviewed Reinboth at his store for about an hour, and then he asked, "Do you have a family?" Yes, Reinboth told him—a wife and two very small children. "Let's go out to the house and visit with them," Bud said, and then he proceeded to spend three hours getting to know Gary, his wife Lois, and the babies. He left, saying, "Let me go back and talk to Brother," his nickname for Sam.

The next night, Sam called to offer Reinboth the job. The Waltons couldn't pay to move the family, but Sam loaned Reinboth $75 to rent a truck. The family pulled into the small town at night. Bud had reserved a hotel room for them and rented one of the few homes available, which was on a gravel road with tall grass and more than a few mice.

The next morning, Bud, his wife Audie, and his father showed up to help clean out the house and move in the Reinboths' belongings. The future store was just brick walls, and Reinboth's first job would be to turn it into a real store. There was one more painful adjustment: Sam took the moving loan out of the first paycheck, a real bite from a monthly salary of just $280.

The St. Robert store opened in October 1964 as a Walton Family Center, and at 13,000 square feet, it was more than twice as big as Sam's original variety stores. Right away, sales took off, building quickly to $2 million a year, far more than any other store in the chain. But keeping enough merchandise in stock was a challenge for such a young company, especially at the busy Christmas season. The second Christmas, shoppers in St. Robert stripped the shelves bare over the weekends. So every other night for a couple of weeks,

Reinboth hitched a trailer to his car and drove more than six hours, with a sleeping wife and two kids, to Arkansas. He stopped at two or three stores in the middle of the night to pick up extra inventory. Then Lois would drive back home while Gary slept.

Though he bought most of his goods from Ben Franklin, Reinboth and his team still had the freedom to try new products. He added men's work clothes—khakis and denim shirts—and they sold out quickly. One of his first employees was Ron Loveless, a young man from Bentonville whose mother once worked as a housekeeper for the Walton family. Sam had recruited him fresh out of the air force to start as a stock boy in the new store. Loveless advanced to pet department manager, where he tested the Waltons' willingness to go an extra mile to satisfy customers.

The department carried a wide assortment of animals—birds, snakes, fish, hamsters, and gerbils—and when one customer wanted a baby leopard, Loveless enthusiastically put in an order. This was no little house cat, however. The leopard ripped up the customer's furniture and, within a week, it was returned for a refund. Loveless donated the cat to a nearby zoo.

Unfazed, Loveless happily took another customer's order for a baby elephant, which sadly died in his crate along the way. Loveless's job almost expired with it.

Reinboth ultimately kept him on, but banned any more exotic animals.

Overall, Sam's chain of stores was good and getting better, thanks in large part to the St. Robert store, which was easily the most profitable one in the chain. The huge sales in this tiny town helped set the future direction of his company. "It turned out that the first big lesson we learned," Sam said, "was that there was much, much more business out there in small-town America than anybody, including me, had ever dreamed of."

Even so, Sam wasn't sitting back and enjoying it. The retail business was beginning to change, and he didn't want to be left behind.

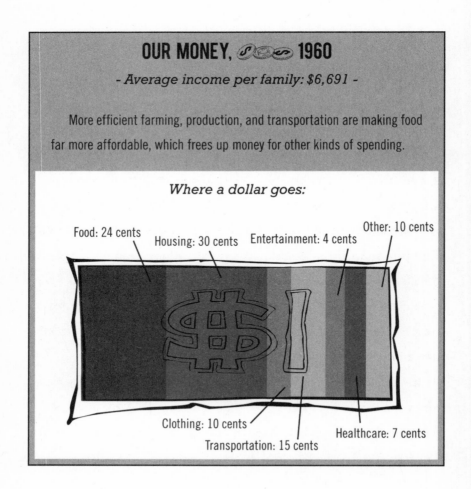

OUR MONEY, 1960

- Average income per family: $6,691 -

More efficient farming, production, and transportation are making food far more affordable, which frees up money for other kinds of spending.

Where a dollar goes:

Food: 24 cents
Housing: 30 cents
Entertainment: 4 cents
Other: 10 cents
Clothing: 10 cents
Transportation: 15 cents
Healthcare: 7 cents

Chapter 5:

Cheap! Cheap! Cheap!

THE KISSY DOLL was *the* toy to get for Christmas in 1961. Dressed in a red gingham dress, she was cute and loving. If you pushed her arms together, her lips would pucker and she would make a kissing sound. Making her more appealing, she was promoted heavily in commercials that ran over and over again during the popular cartoon shows *Bullwinkle* and *Mighty Mouse*.

Stores that sold the Kissy Doll paid a wholesale price of more than $8 a doll to its manufacturer, the Ideal Toy Company. In an ideal world, they would have sold it for a retail price of more than $12, with the $4 markup going toward wages for salespeople and managers, the rent and the light bills, and other store costs, with some left over for a profit.

But 1961 was a year unlike any retailers had ever seen. Discount stores, which had started in the 1940s by stocking manufacturers' rejects and extras, or little-known brands, had evolved during the 1950s as many fair-trade laws fell by the wayside. Now, they were

The TV Star of the year...**KISSY** T.M.

IDEAL'S NEW KISSING DOLL

WHAT A DOLL!

In 1960, Christmas belonged to Ideal's Mr. Machine! This year? Put your money on Ideal's most exciting new doll...KISSY!

There's never been a doll like her. When half a million little girls kiss KISSY this fall you can kiss your worries away. She's got counter-come-on and sales appeal.

The greatest advertising campaign in Ideal's history will have KISSY kissing up a storm of sales for you. She's on two network television shows: Mighty Mouse and Bullwinkle—PLUS thousands of spots in leading kid shows coast-to-coast.

- Kisses when hands are pressed together
- Makes a kissing sound
- Distinctive head with saran-rooted hair
- Arms move—hands turn at wrist
- Dual-purpose "Party and Play" dress

Remember: There is only one "KISSY" Doll And she is made only by IDEAL.

1300-3 KISSY Doll....list price $17.95

U.S. Pat. Pend.© IDEAL TOY CORP.

IT'S A WONDERFUL DOLL...IT'S **IDEAL**   IDEAL TOY CORP., 200 FIFTH AVENUE, NEW YORK 10, N. Y.

Ideal advertised its Kissy Doll in retailer magazines and on television cartoons.

moving into the mainstream, selling big, brand-name products at lower prices. Particularly on the East Coast and in the Midwest, stores were cutting prices and getting a lot of notice. "Battle of the

Karen Blumenthal

Discounters," trumpeted *Time* magazine. "Discount Houses Are Here to Stay," said *BusinessWeek*. *U.S. News & World Report* offered a special report on "A Revolution Under Way in Retailing."

In New York City, selling the Kissy Doll turned into retailing warfare as Christmas approached. By the first week of December, Kissy could be purchased for around $7.50 at both discount and regular stores. Then, one store dropped its price to beat the others, another followed, and within days, the doll could be had for as little as $6.66. The winners were consumers who knew and loved a bargain. But the retailers were losing money by selling toys for less than what they paid so that they wouldn't lose a customer to a competitor, and many feared what was ahead. Already, in New York and other cities, there were smaller price skirmishes on children's snowsuits, men's coats, and other basics.

From tiny Bentonville, Sam Walton had been following the trend and had been visiting some of the new discounters for a few years. A favorite was Fed-Mart, a big discounter on the West Coast that initially served only federal government employees. On the East Coast, the discount leader was E. J. Korvette, which had started out selling luggage and appliances and expanded into selling just about everything else. Sam also visited Ann & Hope, a store started in an abandoned textile mill, and Two Guys from Harrison, which started when two guys from Harrison, New Jersey, began to sell radios and appliances at a discount, and then added housewares. Introducing himself as a country boy from Arkansas, he would strike up a conversation with the managers or owners, trying to

Herb and Belva Gibson, shown holding awards they received from a manufacturers' group, helped pioneer the discount business with a stack-it-high, sell-it-cheap approach.

get as much information as he could about products and prices.

In every way, these stores were a radical change from fancy department stores and plain variety stores like Ben Franklin. Of course, the prices were lower, which meant the store's markup on items was smaller. Physically, the stores were also much larger than variety stores, and carried more merchandise. Unlike department stores, the discount stores were spare in design, without carpet or chandeliers. And they were setting up shop far from the traditional downtown retail district, opening mostly in growing suburbs, where the rents were cheap, major intersections were nearby, and parking was plentiful.

Copying from grocery stores, the discounters offered shopping carts, and purchases were made at a central checkout counter in the front, rather than in each department, reducing the number of clerks

Karen Blumenthal

needed. While discount stores opened at 10 a.m. like the downtown stores and department stores, they stayed opened into the evening; some daring chains were even opening on Sundays, which had long been everyone's day off. (In some states, however, stores weren't legally allowed to open on Sundays.)

Sam was intrigued by the discounters on the East and West Coasts, but he really got interested when Herb and Belva Gibson rolled into his neighborhood. Herb Gibson, a native of Berryville, Arkansas, had started his adult life as a barber and wrestler before becoming a wholesaler to small-town retailers. As the market shifted, he and his wife began to open discount stores, using their skill in buying huge quantities of goods at low prices. Their approach: Stack it high and sell it cheap.

Basing their company just south of Dallas, Texas, the Gibsons opened a few stores and then began selling franchises to local business people, just as the Ben Franklin chain did. In 1959, the first Gibson's opened in northwest Arkansas. It did so well that another one soon opened in Fayetteville, on the same square as Walton's 5 & 10.

The Gibson's outlets stocked 25,000 items. To attract attention, the stores would sell perhaps two hundred popular items at very low prices—at or close to cost. Though other merchandise was priced higher, the deep discounts would leave the impression that everything in the store was dirt cheap. "The public thinks we're giving everything away, and that's what we want them to think," Herb Gibson explained. "It really shakes the town."

When Sam scouted out Gibson's selection and prices, he

immediately saw the potential for his own expanding empire—and what might happen if he ignored this growing competitor. "I wasn't about to sit there and become a target," he decided. He began to map out his own discount store.

A number of the nation's largest chains were see-

ing the same trends. S. S. Kresge (pronounced with a hard "g," almost like Kres-key), a big national variety-store chain, was laying plans for a new chain as well. Kresge's stores were mostly in the downtowns of large cities. As customers moved to the suburbs, sales began to slow and profits slid. Harry Cunningham, the company's visionary leader, concluded that drastic action was needed.

After studying the retail landscape for two years, he was certain that discounting was the solution. He was so confident of his decision that before his first discount store opened, he had lined up more than thirty additional locations. The new chain, to be called Kmart, featured stores that, at 100,000 square feet, would be three to four times bigger than Kresge variety stores. To keep inventory (and costs) lower, they might carry a smaller selection of sizes and brands. But they would also stock everything from silk ties to car batteries. "Our stores are miniature one-stop shopping centers," Cunningham said.

The first Kmart opened on March 1, 1962, in Garden City, Michigan, and seventeen more would open before the end of the year. A department store retailer called Dayton Company in Michigan

Customers line up for the 1962 opening of the first Wal-Mart in Rogers, Arkansas. Right, an ad promotes the grand opening of the third Wal-Mart, in Springdale.

would introduce its first Target store in May 1962, and Woolworth's, another national variety chain, would open its first Woolco in June. All had deep pockets and big plans.

Meanwhile, Sam decided to open his first discount store in Rogers, just down the road from Bentonville. Though Sam had about fifteen variety stores already, they were all tied to Ben Franklin, which meant he got help with merchandise, accounting, and other operations. Opening this discount store was like starting all over again. He had to line up his own suppliers for the merchandise and do many tasks himeslf. That meant he would have to work longer hours and

Mr. Sam

he would need help from additional experienced managers.

Other than his brother Bud, most of his usual investors didn't want to gamble on a new discount store, so Sam turned to banks. Jimmy Jones, a banker at Republic Bank in Dallas, agreed to help fund his further expansion, but at a price: To borrow enough to open the new store, Sam and Helen had to pledge their home and the property she owned through her own family—just about everything they had—to the bank to back the loan.

Choosing a name was a little easier than lining up financing. While on a business trip, Sam asked one of his first store managers, Bob Bogle, for his opinion on naming the store. Bogle's job included buying the variety store signs and he knew how expensive it was to install and light a long name. He suggested something short: "Wal"

Though the Rogers store was expanded and improved early on, displays, like this one for Easter, were very basic, with hand-lettered signs.

for the Walton name and "Mart" for a place to shop. Sam listened, but didn't respond to his suggestion.

A bit later, when Bogle went to check on the new store, he saw a sign man hanging the letters: "WAL—" and realized that Sam had taken his advice. Next to the name, Sam had added two slogans that would become core principles of the company: "We sell for less" and "Satisfaction guaranteed."

The store opened on July 2, 1962—just a few months after the first Kmart, Target, and Woolco—with five hundred people waiting outside for promises of huge savings. The Rogers newspaper noted that the store would feature shopping carts and three checkout lanes, would have parking for one hundred and fifty cars, and would be open from 9 a.m. to 9 p.m. six days a week.

Despite the crowds gathered for the initial sales, it was hardly clear that this would be the beginning of the world's largest retailer. The store's departments were disorganized and it was originally built without a stockroom to hold extra inventory. Sam had to settle for lower-quality merchandise, because big brand names didn't want to cheapen their products by selling to a discounter.

Though Sam was taken with discounting, this first store was just another experiment for him among his other stores and family activities. Helen's Christmas letter for 1962 describes a competitive family with a full schedule. Rob played in the State All-Star football game, graduated from high school, and headed off to the College of Wooster in Wooster, Ohio. John, now sixteen years old, played football and baseball, hunted, and was "dating often." Jim, fourteen, was president of his freshman class, and a football, basketball, and baseball player. And Alice, at thirteen, was competing in quarter horse events, was in the honor society, and had taken fourth place in the state science fair.

Sam, wrote Helen, had recovered quickly from surgery in August in time to participate in a full hunting season; she didn't disclose the problem, though it may have been a hernia caused by lifting something heavy at the house. Her forty-four-year-old husband was moving off the City Council and on to the hospital board. Along with all that, she noted, "Sam and Bud opened the Neodosha, Kansas store, moved two stores to new locations, and opened a discount store at Rogers."

Sometime after the Rogers store was opened, Sam realized that a partner could make the big job of building a discount-store chain easier. He flew to Dallas to see if he could make a deal with Herb Gibson. But Gibson sent him packing.

Sam also went to Chicago to talk to the Ben Franklin executives about the potential of moving into the discount business. But the chain was buying a couple of hundred variety stores with hopes of being a bigger and stronger variety-store chain, and it wasn't interested in Sam's proposal. To move into discounting, Ben Franklin would have to charge less for the merchandise it bought and resold to franchisees like Sam—and it would make far less profit. The executives' answer? No way!

Sam still believed in the concept, and he kept studying others' discount stores, especially when he traveled. On another trip to Ben Franklin headquarters in Chicago, Sam had said hello to Don Soderquist, a Ben Franklin executive. That Saturday, Soderquist was shopping at a Kmart twenty-five miles from the Chicago headquarters when he spotted Sam quizzing a clerk about what the store ordered and how much it bought. At one point, Sam got on his hands and knees to look at the extra goods stored underneath a display.

Finally, Soderquist approached him. "Sam Walton, is that you?" he asked. "What are you doing?"

"Oh, this is just part of the educational process," Sam replied.

Sales at the Rogers Wal-Mart grew quickly toward $1 million a year. But while Sam was tinkering with his store, Kresge was charging ahead with its Kmarts. Thirty-five Kmarts opened in 1963 and more in 1964, ringing up increasing sales. By then, Sam was just getting around to opening his next two Wal-Marts.

One, in Harrison, Arkansas, was a cramped store, about 12,000 square feet, designed for a little town of 6,000. It was spare and, in Sam's words, "truly ugly," but the prices were dirt cheap. Though Sam had high hopes for the grand opening, it made a different kind of impression from the one he had in mind.

David Glass, an executive with a Missouri drugstore chain who would later run Wal-Mart, had heard about the innovative retailer in Arkansas and wanted to see Sam for himself. But what he saw was, he said, "the worst retail store I had ever seen."

"Sam had brought a couple of trucks of watermelons in and stacked

BLACK AND WHITE IN THE 1960s

The late 1950s and early 1960s were a time of racial turmoil in the U.S., and especially in Arkansas. In September 1957, federal troops were called to Little Rock to accompany nine black students to their newly integrated high school after the governor of Arkansas, Orval Faubus, called out the state's National Guard to stop the students from attending. The students eventually were able to complete the year at Central High School, but opposition to integration was so strong that Governor Faubus shut down all of the Little Rock high schools in 1958–59.

On February 1, 1960, four black college students took seats at a Woolworth's lunch counter in Greensboro, North Carolina, and asked to be served. They were turned down, but they politely refused to leave. Day in and day out for six long months, black students and their supporters staged a peaceful sit-in at that lunch counter. Finally, in July, the store desegregated its lunch counter, allowing everyone to eat at any counter or booth.

Both events drew national attention, but they must have seemed like "city" problems to the folks two hundred miles away in northwest Arkansas. The Ozarks, though, had their own serious racial issues.

Up until the late 1950s or early 1960s, a sign on the road between Bentonville and Rogers warned blacks, "You Better Not Let the Sun Go Down on Your Black . . ." followed by a drawing of a donkey, a not-so-subtle reference to "ass." Monte Harris, who grew up in Bentonville, remembers seeing the sign as a high school student and thinking it was just a dumb joke. Only years later, she says, "I realized they meant it."

The message was clear: At least some white residents might try to run off or harm African-Americans who wanted to live in the town or stay after dark. There were hundreds if not thousands of these so-called "sundown towns" across America in the early part of the 1900s, and real violence against blacks prompted many to make their homes in safer places. As a result, there were few people of color at all in many towns.

Bentonville's 1960 population of 3,650 included 21 blacks, mostly household workers and their families. Rogers, where the first Wal-Mart opened in 1962, had only one black resident in 1960 out of 5,700 people. When rhythm and blues singer Fats Domino performed two shows there in January 1962, the *Rogers Daily News* noted that he was the town's "first Negro entertainer." He played to an all-white audience.

Among the first six towns where Wal-Marts went up, only Conway and Fayetteville had sizeable black populations.

As a community leader and variety-store owner, Sam Walton must have been well aware of the histories of Little Rock, Greensboro, and Bentonville. His stores didn't have lunch counters, and they didn't turn away any customers who wanted to shop. Longtime employees say Sam hired blacks from the beginning, though he was slow to promote both women and people of color into upper management. There doesn't appear to be a record of his position on these social issues—he didn't oppose rights and opportunities for blacks, but he didn't stand up or speak out for them, either.

Under the governor's orders, Arkansas National Guardsmen turn away black students from Central High in Little Rock in 1957. Federal troops would later escort the students to school.

them on the sidewalk. He had a donkey ride out in the parking lot. It was 115 degrees, and the watermelons began to pop, and the donkeys began to do what donkeys do, and it all mixed together and ran all over the parking lot," Glass said. "And when you went inside the store, the mess just continued."

Sam seemed like a nice guy, he said, but "I wrote him off. It was just terrible."

Later, Glass realized that he had underestimated a key trait of Sam's: "He has an overriding something in him that causes him to improve every day. That's not difficult when you have something as bad as he had in Harrison, but sometimes you achieve success, and say, 'Boy, now I got it like I want it. Now I can lay back a little and enjoy it.' Sam has never done that. As long as I have known him, he has never gotten to the point where he's comfortable with who he is and how we're doing."

Luckily the other store, in Springdale, Arkansas, got off to a neater start. At 35,000 square feet, it was almost three times larger than the Harrison store, and this time the promotions involved toothpaste at 27 cents a tube and antifreeze at a dollar, instead of watermelons and donkeys. The prices were so low that some customers drove more than an hour from Tulsa to stock up. To help, Sam began checking people out himself, using a tackle box as a cash register.

"After we got those first three stores up and running, I knew it would work," Sam said of his Wal-Mart concept. He opened another one in 1965 and two more each in 1966 and 1967, even while he was still running variety stores under the Ben Franklin and Walton names. He was starting to gain momentum—but though he had nineteen stores in Arkansas, Missouri, and Kansas, his operation was still lean, cheap, and largely run by the seat of his pants.

Since he didn't have a personnel executive, he did much of the recruiting himself. One early manager was a young health department sanitation officer whom Sam had met at the Rotary Club. An early accounting manager was a local accountant who was well regarded. As he visited competing stores and chatted with their managers, he would pull aside those who impressed him and offer them a job. New recruits were encouraged to recommend others.

Often, Sam and Helen visited the recruit's home together, and she would talk with wives and try to sell little Bentonville as a fine place to raise a family. Or he and Helen would host the candidate overnight at their house. Sam didn't care much about the person's education—most weren't college graduates—but he did prefer men who were married and attended church. Why? Sam believed family men had "a certain motivation they wouldn't have otherwise," a family friend explained, and church affiliation "shows they can identify with something outside themselves, that they're willing to work for a common good."

The accounting system was about as haphazard as the hiring process. Sam was still using Butler Brothers' methods, and each month, he and a clerk sat down to tally up each store's sales and expenses. If the math was off, the man who was once sloppy with the paperwork at J. C. Penney didn't spend much time trying to find the reason or the mistake. Instead, he just figured out how much he was off and wrote

Sales and Profits

A retailer's sales are the dollars it receives from selling goods. The money left over after all expenses are paid is called profit. Profits are necessary for a business to grow or improve its operations. A discounter like Wal-Mart has relatively slim net profit, or profit after taxes, about $3.50 for every $100 in sales. That's about half the $6 to $7 a typical company earns on the same sales. Apple, the maker of iPhones and iPods, is a highly profitable company, earning a profit of more than $15 per $100 in sales.

the amount down next to the entry "ESP"—short-hand for Error Some Place.

A lot of merchandise was purchased regionally, and periodically Sam, his brother Bud, and four or five managers would travel together to New York on buying trips, staying three or four to a hotel room to keep costs down. Since Sam was too cheap to spring for cabs, they walked everywhere. Going in pairs, they would head off to buy men's pants or ladies' tops, showing up sometimes before the showrooms opened. There the salesmen would ask what company they were with.

"We're with Walton's," they'd answer.

And where was that?

"Bentonville, Arkansas," they'd tell him.

Nearly always, that prompted another question: "Where in the world is Bentonville, Arkansas?"

And one of the managers would always answer, with a perfectly straight face, "Next to Rogers."

Karen Blumenthal

Only after the salesman had checked the little company's credit-worthiness would he start to negotiate.

By the end of 1967, Kmart was rocking. It had two hundred and fifty stores and more than $800 million in sales, with one hundred more stores in the works. By contrast, Sam was just a blip on the retail radar, with nineteen stores and just $9 million in sales.

But Sam's business was growing, too. Five Wal-Mart stores would open in 1968 and he would keep adding more—if he could find the money. His stores were racking up sales and were plenty profitable,

A display of televisions captivates a young girl at a Kmart in the 1960s.

but building and stocking new ones cost as much as $500,000 apiece. In addition, with so many stores, he had finally agreed with his other executives that the company needed a large distribution center for stocking basic merchandise, so that it could buy bigger quantities at lower prices and deliver them to stores in its own trucks. Also, the executive offices, now above a law office, were beyond cozy. So a distribution center, combined with a modest, warehouselike headquarters, was under construction. But as the company had grown, so had Sam's debt, and borrowing more was becoming a challenge.

In mid-1969, he nearly faced a financial disaster. Retailers often borrow money to open stores, to pay for inventory, or to stock up for Christmas and then repay it after the store opens or holidays end. Needing cash right away, Sam flew to Dallas to draw some money from a standing bank loan. But his old friend Jimmy Jones had switched banks, and his new banker was out of town. He couldn't get anyone at the bank to provide the money he desperately needed.

Distraught and nearly in tears, he phoned Jones at his new bank, National Bank of Commerce in New Orleans. Jones told him to fly to New Orleans and he would be waiting. A bank limousine picked up Sam at the New Orleans airport to whisk him to Jones's office. There, Jones had already prepared the paperwork for a $1.5 million loan. Their long relationship helped Sam sidestep a cash crisis.

But that was no way to run a retailer. If Wal-Mart was to keep growing, Sam knew he would need a better source for money.

Chapter 6:

Going Public!

THE BUSINESS DECISION that Sam faced at the end of the 1960s was as momentous as any he had wrestled with in his twenty-five years of running stores.

The sales rung up by his growing chain were soaring. In the fiscal year that ended in January 1968, sales had been $12.7 million. A year later, they had climbed to more than $20 million, and they were on track to cross $30 million at the end of January 1970, more than doubling in two years.

Profits were expected to nearly double in 1969 alone. But the lack of money to pay for expanding the business had already forced Sam to let go of five properties that might have made great stores. He had borrowed about as much as he possibly could from banks—and to pay that all back, he would need to put the brakes on growth.

Sam and his brother Bud, now a partner in many stores, had few options. They could sell the business to someone else with deeper pockets, but that meant Sam would no longer run the show. Or they

Mr. Sam

could "go public" by selling a part of the company to outsiders—total strangers—who wanted to invest their money in Sam's vision of the discount store.

Small towns welcomed Wal-Mart with newspaper ads and articles, from the 1960s into the 1980s.

For two decades, Sam's stores had been owned by his family and a few managers and partners who might as well have been related for all the hours they spent together. Altogether, fewer than eighty people owned a piece of the eighteen Wal-Marts and dozen Ben Franklin variety stores—including Sam's lawyer, who once asked for some stock instead of cash as repayment for a loan. Sam and Helen and their kids were by far the largest owners, with Bud a distant second.

Selling shares to the public was a complicated and serious process that would change the way the whole business was run. No longer could Sam be creative with his tallies of sales and expenses, simply noting, "Error Some Place." Investors would expect all the figures to be correct and to add up according to formal accounting rules. Each individual store now had a different set of owners; to be a public company, all of the stores would have to be bundled up into one company. More worrisome, selling part of the company to outsiders meant sharing much, much more information, not only about stores and sales, but also about how much Sam and his top executives were paid, what kinds of executive perks they had, and how much of the company stock they owned. It was sort of like opening up their financial clothes closets for everyone to see.

In the fall of 1969, Sam and Bud went hunting on the Robson ranch in Oklahoma, and during a productive day for finding birds, they also weighed their options. They didn't want to lose control of the company, and they weren't even sure that outside investors would want to buy their shares. But an Arkansas investment firm, Stephens Incorporated, had already inquired about helping to sell their stock, so they knew they would get some assistance. On the way home that night, the brothers agreed to seriously explore becoming a public company.

But one partner was strongly opposed. Helen, who had pledged her own family wealth and personal property to help fund the first Wal-Mart, helped hire managers, and participated in many decisions, quite simply "didn't want it to happen."

Over many years, Sam had leaned on Helen for her judgment,

her financial support, and her care. But as the children grew up and the chain grew beyond a family business, Helen had less say in the business. Every time she would think that the chain had grown big enough, Sam would tell her, "Just one more store." Then one or two more stores would be on the drawing board.

"When we got to Wal-Mart, I just said, 'The heck with it. I won't ask again,'" she recalled.

Sam even stymied her efforts to take up flying again. After Alice, their youngest, entered college in 1967, Helen restarted lessons and accumulated about forty solo hours in Sam's single-engine plane. While she was on a trip, Sam upgraded to a twin-engine plane that would require her to have many additional hours of training to fly. But "I couldn't get the plane from Sam," she told an interviewer later, laughing at the memory. "He said what I was doing wasn't business."

Selling stock to the public was a more personal issue for her, and she never fully forgave Sam for going against her wishes. "I always felt we could have gotten by without going public," she said. "Nothing about the company ever affected me as deeply, and it was at that point that I decide to pursue my other interests outside the company. I just hated the idea that we were going to put all our financial interests out there for everybody to see. . . .

"We just became an open book, and I hated it."

Over the years, Sam had hustled to build a team of executives capable of running a growing company. His early managers, mostly high school graduates with retailing experience, had helped start and stock a number of stores, shoulder to shoulder with him. But the stores were getting farther and farther from Bentonville, and to keep everything running smoothly, he needed expertise in building sophisticated systems, like using computers to keep track of all the stuff the stores carried and better methods for handling more complicated finances.

In the mid-1960s, he recruited Ferold Arend, a merchandising expert at a Midwestern competitor, who would soon oversee all store operations. To learn more about the new computers that were being developed, Sam attended an IBM computer school in Poughkeepsie, New York, where he met and began to woo Ron Mayer, a young, aggressive computer and financial whiz who was working for a retailer in Kansas. When he finally convinced Mayer to come take a look at the fledgling Wal-Mart empire a couple of years later, Sam—accidentally—nearly killed both of them.

As he often did with his managers and bankers, Sam put Mayer into his plane to hop around their territory—Arkansas, Kansas, and Missouri—looking at stores. In tiny Carthage, Missouri, the two airport runways intersect. After landing on one runway, Sam's plane was speeding toward the crossing runway when another plane suddenly appeared from nowhere at the intersection.

It was a hair-raising sight. Sam's plane was moving too fast to stop. The other plane was moving way too slowly to get out of the way. Certain disaster was maybe two hundred yards away. With all his might, Sam pushed the levers and made the adjustments to get

Sam often flew his own small plane from store to store, though company pilots began to take over the job in the 1970s.

his plane back in the air. The aircraft trembled and shuddered and wobbled, barely moving off the ground. But then, just as it was coming on the other plane, it rose up, missing an ugly collision by about a foot.

"It was the closest I ever came to getting killed in an airplane," Sam said.

When their hearts settled back into their chests, they continued the tour. After much cajoling, Mayer joined the company in mid-1969 and began to improve how merchandise moved from manufacturers to stores, setting up systems that would allow Wal-Mart to grow faster and more efficiently than anyone had imagined. And he began to help Sam look into how to sell stock to the public.

Sam's oldest son, Rob, had finished law school at Columbia

SAM STORIES: AIR HEAD

As his brother Bud had feared, Sam was about as freewheeling in a plane as he had been in a car. To the horror of his family and co-workers, he regularly skipped important preflight checks, assuming that Wal-Mart's mechanics would keep their planes in good shape.

In the early years, he sometimes picked store locations from the sky, flying low and tilting the plane to look for promising population centers or to count cars in a competitor's parking lot. By the 1970s, though, a company pilot frequently flew the executive, whose piloting style was admittedly a bit too casual for colleagues.

Sam had other close calls beyond the Mayer incident, and in the 1980s, the Federal Aviation Administration actually suspended his license for fifteen days for failing to have the proper training. (He later completed the work.)

Still, Sam loved to fly himself (and his dogs) when he could, frequently setting the plane on autopilot so he could go through his mail or look through computer printouts of sales results to decide which Wal-Mart he would drop in on next. In some of his folksy columns in the company newsletter, *Wal-Mart World*, he would make a point of noting that he was composing the message while traveling on autopilot.

Not surprisingly, passengers weren't always happy about that. Herbert Fisher, the chairman of a New Jersey discount chain, complained one day when Sam turned on the autopilot and turned his attention elsewhere. Sam simply shrugged him off.

"Oh, it's a big sky," he said.

University in 1969 and, setting out on his own, joined a law firm in Tulsa, about two hours away. Wal-Mart would be one of his first clients, and his dad asked him to take care of the legal issues related to the stock sale.

On October 1, 1970, the stock of Wal-Mart Stores Inc. was sold to new investors for the first time. Demand was so high that investors were willing to pay $16.50 a share for each of the 300,000 shares that were offered, more than the $15 a share that Wal-Mart had expected.

That brought Wal-Mart just under $5 million in new money— enough to pay off debts, with some left over to help open new stores.

Once the initial shares were in the public's hands, Wal-Mart stock could be bought and sold among investors in the same way baseball or Pokémon cards are traded after you buy a pack from the store. The stock was so popular on its first day of stock-market trading that investors' demand pushed the price up by $2, to about $18.50 a share.

Sam, now fifty-two years old, and his immediate family were not only debt-free but also undeniably and truly wealthy. Even though they had sold part of the company to new investors, his family still owned about 920,000 shares, or just over 60 percent of the company's 1.5 million outstanding shares. The stock market had put a value on that ownership: $17 million. Bud, forty-nine years old and with a lesser role in the company, owned about 4 percent of the stock, worth more than $1 million. (Other early investors in the stores also now owned valuable shares.)

With the debt worries gone and all the stores formally part of one company for the first time, Sam could expand much faster. He recruited more managers and increased his plans for new Wal-Mart stores while phasing out his Ben Franklin outlets. The stock took off, too. As investors saw how fast this little small-town discounter was growing and how well it was doing, more and more of them wanted to own a part of this Arkansas company. Within six months, the stock price climbed to $46.

At that point, Wal-Mart's board of directors, which watches out for shareholders' interests, decided to "split" the stock, a move that helps keep the price affordable. In some ways, stock splits are a little bit like slicing a pie into smaller pieces. All shareholders receive two shares for every one they own. At the same time, the price of the stock is cut in half to reflect the new shares. So if you owned 10 shares at $46 before a split, you would own 20 shares

RETAIL DETAIL

When a Year Ends in January

In a practice that dates back to the 1930s, retailers typically end their fiscal year, or the period for recording a year of business sales and expenses, at the end of January. That unusual date allows them to include the Christmas selling season of November and December, as well as January clearance sales.

Generally, other company fiscal years end on December 31, but some end on June 30 or other dates. General Mills, the cereal maker, ends its year on the last Sunday in May, a date tied to the harvest of winter grain crops.

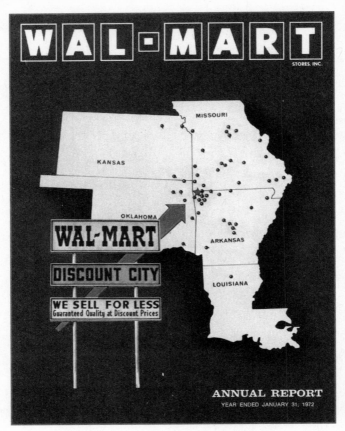

Wal-Mart's first annual report detailed its rapid growth for stockholders.

at $23 afterward—and what you own is still worth $460. Though a stock split seems to be mostly for appearances, shareholders like having more shares, even if they have the same value as the old ones. By the end of January 1972, Wal-Mart had grown to fifty-one stores and sales had more than doubled in two years, jumping to $78 million. The split stock had climbed back from $23 to about $46 a share. Again, Wal-Mart split the stock, and its stock began trading on the prestigious New York Stock Exchange, where the best-run, most-admired companies were trading.

Karen Blumenthal

With so much activity in the stock, another thing was becoming clear. In addition to giving the company the ability to raise money and open new stores, the stock market was creating a huge amount of personal wealth. An investor who bought 100 shares on October 1, 1970 would have paid $1,650. By March 1972, that investor would have 400 shares after two stock splits, and those shares would be worth $9,200.

Early managers were finding that their Wal-Mart ownership had given them riches they never dreamed of having, while Sam's was propelling him into the stratosphere. In 1973, *Fortune* magazine named him one of thirty-nine new "super-rich" Americans, with Wal-Mart stock worth $75 million to $100 million. But though he could buy anything in the world he could possibly want, he was still as cheap—and hardworking—as ever.

From the beginning, he had paid his clerks the minimum amount possible so that he could keep costs and prices low, and in the early 1960s, he had gotten in trouble with the federal government for that. In 1961, the federal government extended minimum wage laws to apply to retail clerks and required stores or chains with sales of more than $1 million to pay their clerks at least $1 an hour in 1961 and $1.15 in 1964. Somewhere in there—the dates are lost to history—the U.S. Department of Labor noted that Sam was buying merchandise for all his stores at once, as though they were part of a chain, requiring him to follow the new rules. Sam argued that each of his stores had different owners, so they weren't really one company or chain. A judge ruled in favor of the government, and Sam raised employees' pay.

A new store in 1972 was larger and neater than early stores, but still bare bones in appearance.

Many years before the company went public, Sam began sharing each store's profits with its manager. But he didn't do that with the average store worker—something he later called "the biggest single regret in my whole business career." Helen pointedly told him that he ought to treat workers a little better, but he didn't fully get the message until the early 1970s, when a union began to make some noise about organizing workers at two stores in Missouri.

Labor unions in the U.S. date back to the late 1800s, when workers banded together into groups so that they would have more power in negotiating with management for higher pay, better hours, or improved working conditions. A union's most potent bargaining chip is a strike, or a refusal to work until workers and management can reach an agreement.

Like many business executives, Sam was deeply opposed to unions. He saw them as divisive, putting a third party between management and employees in a way that hurt communication, raised costs, and made a company less competitive. In response to the murmurings in Missouri, which never advanced to any formal action, he hired an aggressive labor lawyer, John Tate, who had a successful record of keeping unions away. Tate gave him a choice: Sam could either spend a lot of money on lawyers or he could be more generous with his employees. Sam chose the latter, though he and Tate continued to vigorously fight any union-organizing attempts, criticizing unions and arguing that employees would be better off without organizing.

SAM STORIES: OUT OF THE TOILET

Few retail details escaped Sam Walton. He could speak with as much enthusiasm about a store under construction or the company's sales as about the products he was promoting in "Action Alley," the wide center aisle where Wal-Mart featured its weekly specials.

He especially took pride in how managers could take just about any old item and make it a sales superstar with a good display and an enticing price. At various times, minnow buckets, moon pies, and mattress pads would soar in popularity, thanks to a little attention.

Even a plain toilet bowl brush could be an exciting product, he told a retailing group in 1975. By cutting the price to 53 cents from 79 cents and giving the brush prominent display, Wal-Mart could make the household basic an "impulse item," something a shopper bought just because it was an attractive deal. Because of some simple merchandising, he said, each Wal-Mart store was selling about 144 brushes every ten days.

"Sam would be the first to tell you he enjoys making money, but he thrives on merchandising," a good friend and neighbor, Bill Enfield, said. "You should see the way he goes into a store and picks up something—it doesn't matter what—out of one of those bins of his. The way he hold it up, so proudly, and looks at it, it could be the crown jewels."

In 1971, Sam added all kinds of new employee benefits. All workers—clerks, truck drivers, and warehouse help—would share in the company profits, with money set aside based on how much they earned. They would be able to buy Wal-Mart stock at a discount. Sam also came to a realization: If cutting prices meant he sold more goods, sharing profits with employees could mean more profits for all.

Why? "Because the way management treats the associates is exactly how associates will treat the customers," he said.

In his curious and inquisitive way, Sam had always chatted with, quizzed, and helped out clerks and other employees so he would know what was going on, encouraging them to call him Sam, or if they had to be more formal, Mr. Sam. He urged managers and associates to drop the Mr., Mrs., and Miss titles and see each other as part of a team. Later, everyone—Sam included—would wear ID badges with their first names in big letters, an idea Sam picked up at a Texas grocery store.

Early employees remember him stepping in to help bag items for customers, or sitting down with them to help make price tags. He regularly told people how much he appreciated their work, and encouraged others to do the same. "All of us like praise," he said. "We want to let our folks know when they are doing something outstanding and let them know they are important to us."

One of his very first employees back in Newport, Jackie Lancaster, remembered that even at the beginning, Mr. Sam "would praise us for the good job we were doing." But, she said, "He told us never to think that we got so important that we couldn't be replaced."

As his company grew, Sam made a greater effort to let workers know they had a voice in the company, which won him both loyalty and affection. When he visited stores, he sought out clerks to ask them how things were going, how their managers were treating them, and what suggestions they had. He took notes, originally on a legal pad and later with a tape recorder, and he often adopted their suggestions. He had an open-door policy, allowing anyone in the company to come talk to him about a work issue.

Ever since Sam and Helen took a trip to England in the early 1970s, he had taken to calling his employees "associates." (On that trip, he saw a reference to "associates" on a sign, which reminded him how James Cash Penney had called his own employees "associates.") Then, in the mid-1970s, during a trip to Korea and Japan, he saw a rousing company cheer. It was as corny as any idea he ever picked up—asking employees to act like they were at a high-school pep rally—but it was also effective. He rarely visited a store or met with employees without leading them in an energetic version of "Give me a 'W'! Give me an 'A'!"

Sam had always expected his managers to work long hours and wear many hats, but the workweek of a 1970s Wal-Mart executive was equal parts excitement, challenge, and brutal endurance test.

The Wal-Mart executive team in 1973 included Sam (center), Ron Mayer (right of Sam), Ferold Arend (left of Sam), and Bud Walton (next to Arend).

Jack Shewmaker moved to Bentonville with his wife and three small children in 1970 to oversee new store openings and was still unloading the moving van when he was called to go to Missouri to help with a new store. His wife helped him find clothes, and he was off—for two weeks. He had hardly returned when he had to leave again, for two more weeks, for management meetings.

A typical week for a Wal-Mart executive looked something like this: At the Bentonville office on Monday by 6:30 or 7 a.m., in one of Wal-Mart's two or three small airplanes to check out stores or store sites on Tuesday, returning on Wednesday. Thursday was for various meetings, like evaluating new store locations, considering new hires, or making financial projections. Fridays were for merchandise meetings.

Sam's workload was busy, too, but not quite so intense. Still an avid tennis player—and still driven to win—he frequently worked in a match at midday, and he took his racket along on store visits, sometimes asking his secretary to find him an opponent in whatever town he was going to. He was just as serious about quail hunting, often taking his bird dogs on store trips during the winter hunting season so that he could slip away between stops for a little diversion.

From the start, Sam had gathered his top people together early every Saturday morning to go over all kinds of issues, from what was selling to what the competition was doing. Like a determined coach, Sam reminded his people that Wal-Mart was out to win, whether it was up against Kmart, Gibson's, Duckwall, Newberry, Otasco, or some local shop. By this point, that 7:30 a.m. Saturday meeting was a central part of the Wal-Mart culture, putting all the top managers in one room to discuss anything that needed attention.

Other work might be completed on Saturday afternoons. For many Wal-Mart executives, only Sundays were free, so that Wal-Mart men could go to church and spend the day with family. ("We make no bones about the fact that we believe in God, that we think everybody should," Jack Shewmaker once told *Time* magazine.) "That's a pretty hard life," a friend of Sam's noted.

Helen tried to get Sam to let go of the Saturday morning meeting, arguing that headquarters managers should be able to attend their kids' games and activities. But Sam figured that if the store managers and clerks had to work Saturdays, so should the higher-ups.

He would get up at 3 or 4 in the morning to spend two or three hours studying store results so that he would know which stores were struggling, which departments were superstars, and which products weren't moving fast enough. So they wouldn't be upstaged by Sam, the top managers knew they had better get up early and prepare as well.

The meetings were free flowing, without a formal agenda, and they might start with an Arkansas Razorbacks cheer, a loud call of "pig sooooooooeeey!" There were insides jokes, challenges to improve sales or profits or some other business measurement, and sometimes celebrity visitors, like boxer Sugar Ray Leonard, singer Garth Brooks, or former National Football League quarterback Fran Tarkenton.

There were showers of praise for those who did well and cold water for those who didn't, but the critique had to be delivered in a constructive, rather than a personal, way. Al Miles, a former executive, once was especially harsh in criticizing another division and Sam chastised him publicly. "I'll never forget the chairman saying to me one time in front of everybody that I ought to stop and think sometimes before I talked," he said, adding that he deserved the lesson, painful though it was.

Sam also used that time to share his business philosophy, frequently lecturing his key people on keeping costs down at the company and leading frugal lifestyles at home, despite their growing stock fortunes. Sam himself drove a pickup or an older car, and he would tell the executives, "I would hate to see us have a parking lot full of big, extravagant cars." He was clear that he didn't want to see any Lincoln Continentals or Cadillacs or any fancy watches on anyone's wrist. But he was still a small-town boy focused on his growing discount stores, and he wasn't especially savvy about luxury goods.

Ron Loveless, the former stock boy and pet-department manager, had risen through the ranks into management. He had grown up without quite enough to eat and he couldn't resist buying a sports car—a black Porsche, in fact—with money from some of his Wal-Mart stock. One Saturday morning in the middle 1970s, assuming he would arrive long after the boss, he dared to drive his prized possession to work instead of his 1962 Chevrolet.

To his horror, Sam pulled up right next to him.

Loveless braced himself for a lecture, and sure enough, before the meeting was over, Sam launched into one of his passionate frugality speeches. But while railing against fancy big cars, Sam commented that Ronnie had come to work in a new car—but, he added, "it was one of those little economy cars." Loveless's colleagues had to stifle their laughs. Unfamiliar with the model and assuming that all little cars must be inexpensive, Sam had no idea that the Porsche cost far more than a Cadillac.

Sam was even frugal about his own home. In the late 1950s, Helen had decided the growing family needed better quarters, and she hired

Sam and Helen go through their belongings after a fire destroyed the family home.

E. Fay Jones, a University of Arkansas professor and former student of the famous Frank Lloyd Wright, to help design one. The result was a contemporary design, an L-shaped home built over a small creek and waterfall that incorporated rough cedar, native stones, and the local terrain into a serene and stunning home. While it was hardly fancy, it was quite a showcase for Bentonville—although it didn't have central air-conditioning, at least at first. Despite the summer heat, Sam had been too cheap to pay for it.

On a stormy night in April 1972, the home was struck by lightening. Firefighters battled the blaze for three hours, but most of the house was lost. Sam and Helen escaped unharmed, but they virtually

Mr. Sam

had to start over, this time rebuilding for empty nesters instead of for a big family. They put a double-wide trailer on the property, and Helen had to manage the rebuilding because Sam was gone so much. Occasionally, Sam would sit in on the meetings and ask, "Now, Helen, do we really have to do this?"

"Yes, Sam, we do," she would answer.

This time, the house had central air-conditioning.

As Sam and Helen's children grew up, each had to make a decision about how Wal-Mart would fit in their lives. All of the children were owners, all of them had worked at the stores growing up, and Sam let all of them know they were welcome to join the company. One by one, each tried it out.

After helping to take the company public while part of a Tulsa law firm, Rob later joined Wal-Mart at his father's urging. For years, Rob was the company's in-house lawyer, choosing that role rather than one that was more directly involved in operations. John, the second son, had been an All-State tackle on the Bentonville High football team and followed Rob to the College of Wooster, a small Presbyterian school in Wooster, Ohio. But while Rob left after two years to finish up at the University of Arkansas, John quit to join the army—more specifically, the Green Berets, an elite military unit. He served in Vietnam, returning with a Silver Star for heroism during combat. For a short time, he worked as a company pilot, but ended up setting out on his own, running a crop-dusting company and then designing and building racing sailboats.

Jim, the third son, earned a bachelor's degree in business at the University of Arkansas and joined the company in the early 1970s. Working with his uncle Bud in the real-estate department, he learned how to scout for and select store sites and negotiate leases, earning him a reputation as nearly as tight with a dollar as his dad. But after just a few years, he left the company to run Walton Enterprises, which owned the family's Wal-Mart stock and other businesses.

Alice graduated from Trinity University in San Antonio, Texas, in 1971 and worked briefly as a Wal-Mart buyer. But she preferred

Sam and his dogs enjoy a quiet moment outside his rebuilt Bentonville home.

finance, and took a job in New Orleans in banking before working as a stockbroker.

The children were close to their parents, but by the mid-1970s, it was clear that none of them was likely to run the company. Helen began to encourage Sam to cut back from his crazy, demanding schedule. He was working all the time and involved in every part of the business, picking store locations, scouting competitors, studying the finances, and promoting merchandise. But he still loved playing tennis and hunting quail. As he moved into his mid-fifties, he began to think he might pull back a bit and let some of his young guys take over.

Plus, Ron Mayer, now forty years old, was chomping at the bit to run a company. Sam was afraid the man he was relying on for computer and finance expertise might leave if he didn't give him a promotion. So after much consideration, he turned over his chairman and chief executive title to Mayer in late 1974. Sam even switched offices with the new chief to prove that Mayer was now in charge.

Ferold Arend, the store expert, was named president, and Sam became chairman of the executive committee. Sam continued to visit stores and share in big decisions but he was no longer responsible day-to-day.

Under Mayer and Arend, the company continued to rocket forward, adding new stores and racking up increasing sales. The economy was struggling, and customers appreciated Wal-Mart's prices.

But behind the scenes, things were not going well. Cliques were forming, as old-timers lined up behind Arend, and younger, newer managers sided with Mayer.

Sam grew increasingly unhappy about the growing internal conflict. Finally, he couldn't contain himself any longer. On a Saturday afternoon in June 1976, about a year and half after the hand-over, he called Mayer in to say that he was going to take back the top positions. After all, Wal-Mart was still his baby.

Sam encouraged Mayer to stay in a lesser role, but Mayer resigned instead. Inside the company, Sam's reoccupation became known as the "Saturday night massacre." Sam took all the responsibility for the management change.

"I wasn't able to assume a passive role," he said. "The truth is, I failed at retirement worse than just about anything else I've ever tried."

Sam's return was hardly smooth. Several top executives loyal to Mayer followed him out the door, including top financial, data-processing, and distribution-center people.

Sam put together a new team, promoting Jack Shewmaker, a brash but promising store operator, to executive vice president and recruiting David Glass, a longtime drugstore executive, as his financial chief. But after those men were appointed, older executives who had been passed over for promotions departed as well. Altogether, at least six senior executives and several junior executives left, turning over about a third of the top management.

It was a challenging time. Investors began to fret that without that talent, Wal-Mart's rapid growth would stall and its glowing future would dim. The stock price fell.

Even Sam had doubts.

"For the first time in a long time, things looked pretty grim," he said. "And at that point, I have to admit I wasn't sure myself that we could just keep on going like before."

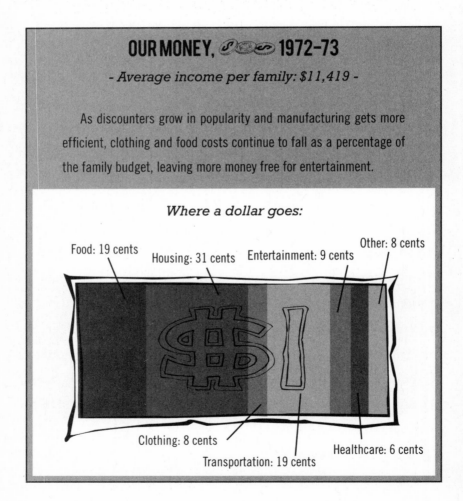

OUR MONEY, 1972-73

- Average income per family: $11,419 -

As discounters grow in popularity and manufacturing gets more efficient, clothing and food costs continue to fall as a percentage of the family budget, leaving more money free for entertainment.

Where a dollar goes:

Food: 19 cents
Housing: 31 cents
Entertainment: 9 cents
Other: 8 cents
Clothing: 8 cents
Transportation: 19 cents
Healthcare: 6 cents

Chapter 7

Grow! Grow! Grow!

WHILE SAM WAS grappling with his internal management challenges, Wal-Mart continued to pack more stores into Arkansas, Missouri, Kansas, and Oklahoma and expand into neighboring states.

With 125 stores and about $335 million in annual sales at the middle of the decade, the chain wasn't yet among the fifteen biggest U.S. retailers. But Sam had a big goal: In 1976 he predicted that Wal-Mart would be a $1 billion company by the end of 1980.

"Write it on the wall now if you want to," he confidently told a reporter.

It was an audacious boast—especially since Kmart, the biggest discounter in the land, was moving into Wal-Mart's strongholds in Arkansas and Missouri. Other regional chains were quaking at the prospect of facing such a giant.

Not Sam. After all, he had spent hours upon hours prowling Kmart store aisles, talking with its clerks, crawling around on its

In the late 1970s, Sam and Helen (right) and Jack Shewmaker (center) cut the ribbon on a new store in Claremore, Oklahoma, Helen's hometown.

floors, and taking notes. He might well have known the stores better than many of its executives did.

"Meet them head on," he told executives of other regional discount chains, who had formed an informal support group. "Competition will make us a better company."

His bluster stood out during a difficult time. There were way too many discount stores, and higher energy costs and inflation, a steady upward creep in prices, were pinching retailers and consumers alike. By the middle of the decade, many chains with names like Mammoth Mart and Giant Stores were going broke.

By focusing on towns as small as 5,000 people and small cities within a territory he called the "magic circle," Sam, however, had most of his markets to himself. For years, Wal-Mart had been filling in and expanding this circle, so named because Bentonville and its warehouse were at the center and each store was within an easy day's drive, allowing shelves to be restocked frequently.

Wal-Mart's arrival in these towns was often front-page news and a cause for celebration, a sign that a town had a certain cachet. Mayors, business leaders, and local beauty queens happily turned up at the grand opening to welcome a bigger store with lower prices. The main competitors were local mom-and-pop stores, which, with their smaller spaces, shorter store hours, downtown locations, and higher costs, were hardly a match. With so little real competition, Sam's financial results stood out all the way to Wall Street.

Walter Loeb, who researched and followed Wal-Mart for the New York investment firm Morgan Stanley & Co., calculated that a Wal-Mart store could generate annual sales of a stunning $1,000 per inhabitant in the small towns it entered because people did so much of their shopping there. The stores didn't just serve one town but drew customers from communities as far as twenty miles away.

Sam was also perfecting the management style that would make him famous, obsessively visiting his stores and stopping in at competitors' stores nearby, searching for retail trends. He was so curious about others' operations that he kept his last Ben Franklin variety store well into the 1970s so he could see what merchandise the Ben Franklin folks were buying. No matter what another store looked like or how poorly it was run, Sam could nearly always find something interesting to note and share later.

Once, on a visit to a Huntsville, Alabama, competitor, Sam and

Don Soderquist, who had joined Wal-Mart from Ben Franklin, scouted the aisles separately. When they met up in the parking lot, Sam asked Soderquist a question he asked often: "What do you think?"

Soderquist had nothing nice to say. The store was dirty, rows of shelves were empty, and no one was around to help. "Sam, that was the worst store I have ever seen in my life," Soderquist said. "What did you think?"

"Did you see the panty hose rack?" Sam replied. "That was the best panty hose rack I have ever seen. We don't have one that looks half as good as that one." Sam was so impressed that he had pulled out the fixture and written down the name of the maker.

A *Forbes* reporter, noting that fifty-nine year old Sam tried to visit every Wal-Mart twice a year, followed him on a swing through Missouri. Meeting first with a group of associates in Cameron, Sam was quick to praise them, saying, "I'm really impressed with the way you've got things set up in those departments. You're the people who really make us a success."

In the notions area, the department manager told Sam that she sold more fabric folded than on bolts, a tip he would pass on later. He apologized to a woman running the consumer electronics counter for not giving her enough staff. "We made a mistake," he said. And he frowned at half-empty shelves in the automotive area, encouraging the store manager to find a better way to keep products in stock.

In Chilicothe, he admired a Count Dracula Halloween

SAM STORIES: BACK TO NEWPORT

Nearly twenty years after he had been run out of his Ben Franklin store in Newport, Arkansas, Sam returned, opening a Wal-Mart in 1969. "By then, I was long over what had happened to us down there, and I didn't have revenge in mind," he said later.

Or did he? Former managers remember that he cared deeply about the store's performance. He also embellished the story over the years, making it appear that Wal-Mart was more successful there than it was.

Because a local factory had closed just as the store opened, the big, new Wal-Mart didn't have many shoppers. Ron Loveless, the first manager, cut his staff to the bone, but labor costs as a percentage of sales were still higher than they were supposed to be.

Late one Saturday night, Sam called him, demanding to know why his costs were out of whack. Tired, and frustrated, Loveless ended the call by hanging up on his boss.

At 4 a.m., a Wal-Mart executive woke up Loveless with a knock and a stern message: Sam wanted the manager fired. Over coffee in his kitchen, Loveless agreed to apologize and was transferred to a smaller, but higher-volume store.

The Newport Wal-Mart eventually turned around, though the local Ben Franklin hung on for years, remaining on the square until the late 1970s.

That's not Sam's version. "We did extraordinarily well with our Newport Wal-Mart, and it wasn't too long before the old Ben Franklin store . . . had to close its doors," he said in his autobiography. Still, Sam insisted, Wal-Mart didn't kill the Ben Franklin.

"His customers were the ones who shut him down," he said, an argument he would make many times as Wal-Mart grew bigger and more powerful.

Sam tours Missouri stores in 1977.

promotion; in Excelsior Springs, he was wowed by the houseplant display. Harrisonville won his biggest praise, however, because it had a full selection of automotive supplies and the other stores didn't. Just as in the early days, keeping key items in stock still mattered.

As far as Sam was concerned, there was plenty of growth in this modest slice of Middle America. "There's no need to go out of our region," he told the reporter. "There are at least 400 new locations waiting for us where we are, enough for eight or ten years."

Even as he made that prediction, however, Wal-Mart was building a new distribution center on the east side of Arkansas, which would allow it to push farther into the Southeast. Taking advantage of a competitor's woes, it acquired fourteen Mohr Value stores and added a total of forty-two stores in the fiscal year ending in January 1978. Thirty-four more were added the next year. The growth was so fast and furious that the new distribution center was pressed into service before the roof was finished.

With all of Wal-Mart's rapid expansion and its impressive results, Sam wasn't paying enough attention to important details. He got a wake-up call when he asked a group of retail executives from other parts of the country to come down to his territory and give him an honest review of his business. They toured several stores and their list of shortcomings went on and on: Signs were awful. There was too much of some categories and not enough of others. The stores were a crowded mess. In addition, prices on some items were too high. "What they had to say really shocked us," Sam said.

Sam and his executives took the critical review to heart. Chains like Target, with its big city and suburban stores, had been raising the bar, carrying mostly brand-name goods and ditching messy tables and piles of merchandise for displays like those in a department store. Sam and Shewmaker asked their executives to look more closely at competitors coast to coast for ideas that Wal-Mart might adopt.

Out of that, they built two experimental stores, dropping a dark blue and white color scheme for a softer palette of light beige, soft blue, and burnt orange and adding carpet to the apparel departments. With discount stores far more commonplace and attracting far more consumer dollars than in the 1960s, they were now able to bring

SAM STORIES: WALTON FAMILY ENTERPRISES

Retailing wasn't Sam's only business interest. In the early 1960s, the tiny Bank of Bentonville, with just $3.5 million in assets, hit a rough spot. At the urging of Jimmy Jones, the banker who would later help finance Wal-Mart, Sam bought it, giving him some insight into how banks and lending worked.

Over time, Sam added other small, local banks in northwest Arkansas to his portfolio, and as his wealth grew, he personally invested in other ventures, such as a grocery store.

In the 1970s, Wal-Mart bought the *Benton County Democrat*, the twice-a-week newspaper in Bentonville, so that it would have printing presses for its advertising circulars. When Wal-Mart's needs grew too big for the small paper's presses, Sam's son Jim formed a new company, Community Publishers, Inc., with a business partner and bought the paper in 1982.

All of the businesses operated under the umbrella of Walton Enterprises, the company that also owned the family's Wal-Mart stock. For a time, that made Bentonville the ultimate company town, a place where Sam Walton and his family controlled the biggest company, the local bank, the newspaper, and some other businesses.

Community Publishers sold the Bentonville paper in 2005, but still owns more than twenty small newspapers and community Web sites in the region. The banking company, now called Arvest Bank, owns sixteen banks in four states and has more than $10 billion in assets.

in—and discount—more brand names that customers wanted, like Wrangler jeans, Pioneer electronics, and Revlon cosmetics, which replaced the generic, and often more profitable, items they had been carrying. Taking what they learned from those stores, Wal-Mart began to gussy up—and just in time.

While Sam was opening a few dozen stores a year, Kresge, led by its Kmart division, was growing much faster. In 1977, the year Kresge changed its name to Kmart Corporation, the chain saw sales surge past $9 billion, making it the nation's third largest retailer, behind Sears, Roebuck and the large grocery chain Safeway. The next biggest discount chain, Woolco, was barely one-fourth its size.

When Kmart rolled into Little Rock, facing Wal-Mart head on, the little chain was ready. Store managers were told that, no matter what, Kmart's prices couldn't be lower than its own. As both stores fought for business, the price of a tube of Crest toothpaste fell to 6 cents.

Wal-Mart held its ground in Little Rock and beyond—in large part because of decisions it had made along the way. Early on, Sam committed to remodeling or expanding each physical store every few years, so Wal-Mart's older stores were in good shape. Fast-growing Kmart had not, and its assortment of cheap, generic clothing won it the nickname "the Polyester Palace."

Though Sam hated spending money, he purchased expensive technology at the urging of other executives. Wal-Mart began computerizing its ordering system in the early 1970s, which allowed stores to send in orders to headquarters over phone lines, so head-quarters could quickly relay orders to vendors. Wal-Mart added elec-tronic cash registers in the middle of the decade, and a few years later, experimented with a new idea, striped stickers called bar codes. Cashiers could scan the bar code and the price would show up on the register; even better, the computer could track how well each item was selling and let store managers and headquarters know how much to order and when. Kmart managers, however, were still sending in orders to headquarters by mail.

Kmart was so much bigger than Wal-Mart, though, that the dif-ferences weren't yet apparent, and Kmart executives were almost cocky about their size. They bragged about selling film and tooth-paste at super-low prices to bring in traffic, luring in male shoppers (who were notorious for buying on an impulse) with strong sporting goods and automotive departments, and trying to provide just about anything a family could need.

Harry Cunningham, who had led the company into the discount business, had handed over the reins in 1972, but he was still confi-dent about his creation. "Nothing can stop Kmart," he told *Fortune* magazine in 1977.

Clearly, he wasn't paying enough attention to the scrappy retailer in Bentonville, Arkansas. Sam had started 1970 with just thirty-two stores, bringing in $31 million. By 1980, he had 276 stores from Texas to Alabama and as far north as Illinois. Sales had climbed to $1.2 billion—more than meeting his boast of a few years before.

His company was only the eighth-largest discounter in the U.S., but a Wall Street analyst predicted that if any chain could challenge Kmart, "the best guess is that it would be Wal-Mart." Two trade magazines, *RetailWeek* and *Discount Stores News*, already had named Sam "Retailer of the Year." Yet, many people outside of the South had never heard of him.

He wouldn't be anonymous much longer.

Chapter 8

Rich, Richer, Richest!

SAM LOVED CHANGE—thrived on it really—so much so that he laughed at the idea that he had a grand plan for building Wal-Mart. He was so quick to follow the next idea that he could hardly keep an appointment. Though his secretary, Loretta Boss Parker, kept two calendars (one for him and one for her), there were times when someone would fly in to meet Sam, and she would discover that Sam had flown out of town early that morning without telling anyone.

Eventually, she told him he should make his own appointments. "Then," she said, "he would make his own appointments and forget about them, and I was still the one who had to give them the bad news."

That flexibility allowed Sam to respond quickly to competition. But in the early 1980s it would be challenged by two unexpected curveballs—one personal and one from a national magazine.

Neither of those developments could have been anticipated in

1980, though, when Sam must have felt like Wal-Mart was a winning team just on the verge of greatness. Jack Shewmaker, the president and chief operating officer, and David Glass, the chief financial officer, had passed their initial tests with flying colors and were breaking new ground. A painful economic recession that resulted in the highest U.S. unemployment rate in a generation made his stores' low prices more attractive than ever.

Meanwhile, the one-two punch of inflation and a bad economy was demolishing less-disciplined competitors. The original discounter, Korvette's, closed for good. Gibson's was a shadow of its former self. J. C. Penney gave up on its discount experiment and before long, Woolworth's would throw in the towel on Woolco, a discount

Sam was just as aggressive on the tennis court as in business.

chain of more than three hundred stores that once had been a distant number two to Kmart.

In that miserable environment, Wal-Mart was a genuine retail success story—one of the very few in the country—and Wall Street was in love. The stock price surged and Wal-Mart split the stock again, for the fourth time since the company had gone public. A person who had purchased 100 shares back in 1970 for $1,650 now would have 1,600 shares worth about $40,000.

Even company clerks and truck drivers were benefiting. Thanks to the profit-sharing program Sam had started in the early 1970s, a portion of the company's profits were set aside for every employee who had been there at least a year. Because the money was invested in Wal-Mart stock, those profit-sharing accounts climbed when the stock price rose. Some longtime employees had accumulated tens of thousands of dollars in their accounts, a perk that made up for modest wages.

Further, with little debt and fattening profits, Wal-Mart could take advantage of a competitor's woes. One troubled retailer was Kuhn's Big K, a chain based in Nashville, Tennessee, that had more than one hundred discount stores just to the east of Wal-Mart's territory. Sam was friendly with the Kuhn brothers, Jack and Gus, and in an old-fashioned, unspoken agreement, Sam had stayed out of the Kuhn brothers' territory and they had stayed out of his. Until, that is, Sam ran out of room in Arkansas and Missouri. Then, Sam moved into Tennessee, and the Kuhn brothers, in response, opened stores in Arkansas.

SAM STORIES: GREETERS

The "greeter" is a familiar sight in the front of a Wal-Mart store, often a senior citizen in a Wal-Mart vest who greets customers and offers assistance.

Sam was a big champion of greeters. He liked the way they made people feel welcomed. But he also liked their other purpose: to reduce shoplifting.

The idea came from a Wal-Mart store in Crowley, Louisiana, that had a problem with stolen goods walking out the door. To cut the shoplifting, the manager stationed an older person at the door, believing a friendly greeter would be less intimidating to honest customers than a security guard.

Sam fell for the idea as soon as he saw it. For years, he had worked to reduce "shrinkage," the loss from customer and employee theft. Wal-Mart even paid small bonuses to employees whose stores kept their shrinkage below the company's goals. Greeters would only help that effort.

For months, Sam urged every store to add a greeter. But the company always encouraged debate, and many managers and executives pushed back, saying they thought the position was a waste of money. Sam was relentless, and eventually he got his way. His real vindication, however, came later, when Kmart and other stores added greeters of their own.

But while Sam was thriving, Kuhn's was losing money. Sam wrestled with the decision to buy the Tennessee chain. If the move was right, Wal-Mart would quickly become one of the nation's biggest discounters. But if Sam and his team couldn't efficiently convert the stores to profitable Wal-Marts, it could end up as troubled as Kuhn's itself.

Finally, in December 1980, he agreed to buy the company for about $17 million. The next month, he backed out because Kuhn's hadn't been able to rework some store leases. In June 1981, he agreed to buy Kuhn's again, this time for about $13 million, and he included a clause that he could cut that price if Kuhn's troubles got worse.

They did—and Sam got a bargain better than any in his discount aisles. He paid $7.5 million, less than half of what he had originally offered. After closing a few stores, he added ninety prime locations and two new states to the Wal-Mart juggernaut for a fraction of what it would have cost to open them himself. Kuhn's had little choice but to accept it.

Energized by the Kuhn's purchase and the twentieth anniversary of that first messy Wal-Mart store in Rogers, Arkansas, Wal-Mart revved up its store expansion and hired hundreds of former discount-store managers and employees to help staff its new stores. By early 1982, after opening more than sixty additional Wal-Marts, Sam had nearly five hundred stores in just thirteen states, and more than 40,000 employees. Having more than doubled his sales in just two years, he was now the second-largest discount chain in America. Finally, there were no other discounters between Wal-Mart and Kmart.

★ ★ ★ ★

Karen Blumenthal

Though now sixty-four years old, Sam was as com-
mitted as ever to nurturing his baby—but he was having a hard time
doing it. He just wasn't feeling well. For months, he had been tired,
unusually so. At Helen's urging, he cut back on his travel and tried to
play more tennis and hunt more often. But that wasn't helping.

Finally, he went to the doctor, who discovered his white blood
cell count was unusually low. Further tests showed he had a chronic
form of a rare cancer, hairy-cell leukemia, which probably had been
developing for a few years.

Given his busy life and the fact that Sam's mother died of cancer,
this had to be frightening diagnosis. But the man who was outgoing
and friendly with associates was unusually tight-lipped about personal

Former President Jimmy Carter was one of Sam's hunting partners in the mid-1980s.

matters, and if it upset him, he didn't let on. He doesn't mention the leukemia at all in his autobiography, though he did share the news in the company newsletter in October 1982, saying he wanted to avoid a lot of rumors. But he was typically upbeat.

"We've always believed in communicating with one another for better or for worse, and in being up front and open with most everything that affects our Company," he wrote. He said his condition was "not of serious proportions" and was slow-growing. He added that he was "completely confident" that treatment would allow him to be around another twenty or twenty-five years. He was looking forward to visiting more stores, playing more tennis, bird hunting, and even taking more vacations with Helen. He also made clear that he wouldn't put up with "sympathy or undue conversation concerning my health."

In other words, he didn't want to talk about it. And for quite some time, little else was said. Though Wal-Mart and Sam Walton were tightly intertwined, the company didn't mention his illness in reports to stockholders, even though publicly traded companies are supposed to reveal information that might affect the company's prospects or stock price. In a rare mention in the press, a *BusinessWeek* story in late 1985 noted that the stock had dropped sharply when the word leaked out. But it recovered quickly. The story said the "condition was arrested with only a change in diet."

The treatment was actually far more complicated. The cancer wasn't life-threatening yet, but it had the potential to worsen. Meeting with doctors at M. D. Anderson Hospital in Houston,

Texas, Sam was as inquisitive and controlling about his treatment as he was about store merchandise. A new drug called interferon was being tested and showed promise, though it was hard to get and very expensive. Sam peppered the doctors with questions and took some time to decide whether he wanted to try it.

In the first year after his diagnosis, Sam was in and out of the hospital. Tests showed his bone marrow was full of leukemia cells, and he was feeling low. As luck would have it, scientists figured out a way to make a synthetic interferon. It was still new and untried, but it would be more readily available than the previous medicine. His doctor was enthusiastic about the possibilities, and Sam began getting interferon shots in the fall of 1983, daily at first and then less often.

The shots not only had few side effects but also were remarkably effective. In the fall of 1984, Sam wrote in his chairman's message in *Wal-Mart World* that he was now in remission, though he would continue the interferon for some time. He would remain in partial remission for years, regularly visiting his Houston doctors, while nearly always making time to visit stores when he was there.

Despite Sam's insistence that he didn't want any fuss over him, Bentonville threw an elaborate Sam and Helen Walton Appreciation Day in 1983. The newspaper, now owned by son Jim and a partner, produced a special section detailing his life. A main thoroughfare was renamed Walton Boulevard, a new junior high was named after Sam, and a new nonprofit daycare center had Helen's name on it.

Sam and Helen were honored with a parade featuring school and university marching bands, drill teams, and several floats. One favorite: a smashed-up car attached to the back of a Wal-Mart truck. That float commemorated the day in 1981 when Sam crashed into the back of a Wal-Mart truck while trying to count cars in a competitor's parking lot. Luckily, only egos were bruised—especially that of the truck driver, who had just received a ten-year safe driving award.

A dinner and roast followed the parade, attended by both United States senators from Arkansas and then-governor Bill Clinton, and featuring a congratulatory call from President Ronald Reagan. Though Sam must have been undergoing cancer treatment at the time, his illness doesn't appear to have been mentioned, not in the special newspaper section, in his and Helen's speeches, or in any news accounts of the day.

Perhaps to keep attention focused on the company, or maybe just to push folks a little harder, in 1983 Sam also made a daring challenge to employees: He wanted the company to earn a pretax profit of eight cents on every dollar of sales for the company's fiscal year ending in January 1984. This was an almost outrageous goal—even as penny-pinching as Wal-Mart was, it earned at best a pretax profit of six to seven cents for every dollar of sales, which was considered very high for a business so focused on low prices.

"You'll never do it," Sam told company executives. "If you do, I'll do the hula on Wall Street."

He wasn't kidding. Making silly bets and holding people to them were part of the company culture. Drawing on its small-town roots, stores sponsored pretty baby and moon pie–eating contests and theme days, when employees dressed up. Executives regularly challenged each other to pass goals. Shewmaker had put on a grass skirt and done a Hawaiian dance at a store, and Glass had recently done the hula for Bentonville employees when the stock hit a new high. Still, Sam thought his day would never happen.

Egged on by Sam, employees worked hard to cut expenses in every way, actually hitting that lofty goal. So on a blustery cold day in March 1984, with temperatures below freezing, Sam found himself in front of the Merrill Lynch Building in New York City. To call attention to his boss and the achievement, David Glass arranged for real hula dancers and a ukulele player to accompany Sam, and alerted

In one of his most embarrassing moments, Sam does the hula on Wall Street to pay off a bet he made with employees.

newspapers and television stations. While passersby stopped to stare, Glass helped Sam don a grass skirt, a Hawaiian shirt, and a couple of leis over his pin-striped suit.

Though Sam had long been a something of a promoter, energetically entertaining employees, shareholders, and store customers, he suddenly felt uncharacteristically ridiculous. As cameras snapped and the music played, he did the best sixty-five-year-old-company-executive hula dance he could muster. It was, reviewers noted, a bit on the stiff side. "It was one of the few times one of our company stunts really embarrassed me," he confessed later.

The summer of 1984 was a time of more change.

Sam's father Tom, whose work ethic had been a steady influence in his son's life, passed away at age ninety-two in Columbia, Missouri. The usually upbeat Sam was deeply saddened. He hung his father's cane on his office wall, and he and Bud donated $150,000 to Columbia for a new visitor's bureau named in honor of Thomas G. Walton.

Sam also began to prepare for the inevitable day when a new leader would have to take over. He asked Shewmaker and Glass to switch jobs, saying that the two contenders for the top job needed to understand all parts of the business. But others believed that he was just pitting them against each other, like making two quarterbacks compete for the position.

The two couldn't have had more different personalities. Shewmaker, a friend and occasional hunting buddy of Sam's, was a

Sam regularly visited stores and helped with celebrations, like this 1984 store opening in Springdale, Arkansas.

brilliant merchant who was credited with making "everyday low pricing" a key strategy; by weaning the company from promotions and clearance sales, he enabled Wal-Mart to cut its advertising costs, save on the cost of changing prices, and reassure customers that good deals would always be there. But despite his creativity, Shewmaker could be cocky, blunt, abrasive, and hard on underlings. He also had a prickly relationship with Rob Walton, who likely would represent the Walton family after Sam. By contrast, Glass was analytical and calmer under pressure, an adept administrator and better at delegating. But he was so reserved that he seemed to completely lack charisma.

To outsiders, the two were equals, with the same salary, the same

amount of time to speak at managers' meetings, and equally important jobs. But to insiders, Sam's decision to put Glass in charge of
operations meant Glass was all but wearing the crown. Since Sam
wasn't ready to retire, the two would work side by side for several
years before a final decision would be made.

In the meantime, thanks to the hula and the management change,
people were beginning to notice Wal-Mart's impressive expansion, its
skyrocketing stock price, and its just-one-of-the-guys leader. With so
many new stores, and sales climbing so fast, the stock had doubled
in price and then tripled. The company declared stock splits in both
1982 and 1983. A person who bought 100 shares in 1970 would, by
early 1985, have 6,400 shares, worth roughly $300,000. Longtime
employees now had fortunes in their profit-sharing accounts that
exceeded their wildest expectations.

And Sam? The percentage of stock he owned in Wal-Mart fell
in the 1970s as the company sold more shares. But he still had about
40 percent and was wealthy almost beyond words. Thanks to *Forbes*
magazine, the whole world now knew it.

In 1982, *Forbes* had launched a hugely popular annual feature
naming the four hundred richest Americans. The issue fascinated
readers, generated news stories, and provoked anger from those
on the list, who worried about their safety and about being bom-
barded with requests for money. In the first issue, *Forbes* had tagged
Sam and his family at number seventeen, with $690 million. But as
Wal-Mart's stock soared, Sam moved to number two, after oil heir
Gordon Getty.

SAM STORIES: OL' ROY

Sam loved quail hunting, so much so that during hunting season, he took his dogs along on trips, hoping to squeeze in a hunting break between store visits.

What he loved most wasn't knocking birds down from the sky, but training and working with his dogs. "I just thoroughly enjoy the partnership that develops between a hunter and a bird dog," he explained. "I enjoy getting these new pups and turning them into bird dogs."

In the 1970s, Sam grew attached to one dog more than the others. Roy slept with him in hotel rooms while the other dogs stayed in the car. He went on store visits and to managers' meetings. Sam frequently shared Roy stories in his *Wal-Mart World* column.

Jana Jae, a singer and fiddler, recalled that during one managers' meeting, she started to play, and Roy headed to the stage. "He had a reputation for decorating the hallways, so all the managers watched to see what he'd do," Jae said. As she played, the dog joined her on stage and started howling to the music.

When "Ol' Roy" died in 1981, Sam wrote in the company newsletter that he had shared some of his most pleasurable hours with his dog. He also named Wal-Mart's dog food after his pet, adding to the package, "Mr. Sam Walton's Bird Dog, Ol' Roy, 1970–1981. Gone but Not Forgotten." In part because of Wal-Mart's size, the brand became the best-selling dog food in America.

But Ol' Roy, it turned out, wasn't all that good at his original job, bird hunting. He was better at finding rabbits than quail and much better at fetching tennis balls. "Roy was probably the most overrated bird dog in history," Sam admitted later.

Sam with Ol' Roy.

Then, in the fall of 1985, just after Wal-Mart's stock split yet again, for the seventh time in its fifteen-year history as a public company, *Forbes* named him the richest man in America. His fortune, nearly all in Wal-Mart stock, was an estimated $2.8 billion—enough to spend $1 million a week for more than fifty years.

Reporters rushed to Bentonville to profile the new king of capitalism, who had made his money not by inheriting it or striking oil or inventing something, but by building a business store by store, selling cheap socks, panties, and toothpaste. In this little backwoods Ozark town, they were amazed to find that America's richest man was, shockingly, a lot like the rest of us. He drives an old pickup truck—himself! He has coffee every morning at the

Even as America's richest man, Sam worked in a simple, windowless office (recreated at the Wal-Mart Visitor Center).

local coffee shop! He flies coach on commercial airplane trips! He pays $5 for a haircut at the barbershops because, well, that's what the barber charges in Bentonville. (And he doesn't tip!) He dines on Friday nights on the barbecue chicken or the filet at Fred's Hickory Inn, where he tips 15 percent. (His brother Bud, however, tips 20 percent.) Sure, he owns a plane, but he bought it used!

The *Washington Post* told the story of Jamie Beaulieu, a twenty-three year old hired to help serve food at Sam's birthday party. Jamie wore a tuxedo, expecting to go to a mansion, and to see servants and at least one Rolls Royce. Instead, he saw the Walton's rustic stone and glass home, the old truck, and a muddy bird dog.

"It was a real letdown," he said.

Reporters were often disappointed by Wal-Mart's spare and sprawling warehouselike offices, as though they expected a glass-and-steel high rise in Bentonville, with its population of about 10,000 people. The lobby, with its plastic chairs and coffee vending machine, was so unimpressive that *BusinessWeek* once described it as "Early Bus Station." Sam's modest office wasn't much better: It had wood paneling and no windows.

The reporting frenzy frustrated Sam, too. While he didn't mind the money—and he was certainly willing to spend it on the best medical care, family gatherings at fancy resorts, and desirable hunting leases—it wasn't that interesting to him, and he genuinely hated just about any kind of media attention. Instead, his passion was

Wal-Mart and its remarkable run. That's what he had spent his life building.

"It's not money. It's all paper," he said of his wealth. And, in fairness, a good bit of it was. The family did own a banking company and a small newspaper, and received Wal-Mart dividends, or a portion of profit paid to stockholders. Most of his fortune, though, was tied up in Wal-Mart stock, and its value would bounce around with the company's successes and failures and with the stock market. To have the really big bucks in his pocket, he would have to sell some of his stock. Doing that would reduce his control in the company, something that wasn't about to happen.

Just as in the early 1970s, Sam still believed that both he and Wal-Mart executives should save the company money and be careful with their own funds. On business trips, Wal-Mart employees still stayed in modest hotels two to a room, they always flew coach, and once airlines started frequent-flier miles programs, the miles stayed with the company, not the traveler.

Sam still got lathered up about lavish living. "Maybe it's none of my business, but I've done everything I can to discourage our folks from getting too extravagant with their homes and their automobiles and their lifestyles," he said. "Every now and then somebody will do something particularly showy, and I don't hesitate to rant and rave about it at the Saturday morning meeting. . . . I don't think that big mansions and flashy cars are what the Wal-Mart culture is supposed to be about."

Sam tried to cool the fevered interest in him and his money after the *Forbes* story by refusing nearly all interview requests. The private family became even more so. But rather than tamping down the growing fascination, this made him more intriguing and mysterious. In fact, as he got richer and Wal-Mart got bigger, they both began to draw more and more attention of a very different kind.

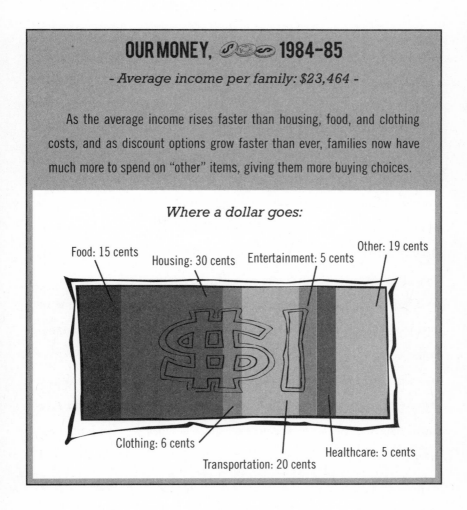

OUR MONEY, 1984-85

- Average income per family: $23,464 -

As the average income rises faster than housing, food, and clothing costs, and as discount options grow faster than ever, families now have much more to spend on "other" items, giving them more buying choices.

Where a dollar goes:

Food: 15 cents
Housing: 30 cents
Entertainment: 5 cents
Other: 19 cents
Clothing: 6 cents
Transportation: 20 cents
Healthcare: 5 cents

Chapter 9

Go! Go! Go!

THOUGH HIS HAIR was white and thinning and he was moving into his late sixties, Sam Walton embraced his advancing years with a burst of energy and creativity.

Wal-Mart was still growing by leaps and bounds, adding well over one hundred stores a year. By 1985, annual sales were approaching $5 billion, though the company was still in only twenty states, mostly in the South, and was just venturing into Colorado and Wisconsin.

Until 1983, Sam had put nearly all of his energy into his Wal-Mart stores. He had experimented with a building-supply and home-improvement store in Rogers called Save-Co in the mid-1970s, but it wasn't successful and he closed it in 1977. (Coincidentally, the first Home Depot opened its doors the next year.) In the early 1980s, he was captivated by deep-discount warehouse clubs that were starting to spring up. The first such store, Price Club, began in California and catered to small businesses, such as restaurants or car-repair shops, which previously had bought basics like toilet paper or sodas from different suppliers and not always at low prices. To shop at Price Club, however, small businesses or others had to pay a membership fee. After visiting Price Clubs several times, Sam decided that such a store would fit with Wal-Mart's strengths in discounting and buying in big quantities and would give his company a new avenue for growth.

Sam's Club, a gigantic warehouse club that sold only super-size quantities at near-wholesale prices to members, opened its first store in 1983, and by the mid-1980s, it was moving out of the test phase to become a key part of the company. Eleven of these bare-bones stores were open, mostly in or near bigger cities, and another ten to twelve were on the drawing board.

The new store, Sam said, "was almost what you'd call a second

The first Sam's Club, then called Sam's Wholesale Club, opened in Oklahoma City, Oklahoma.

childhood for me—a second challenge anyway. I had a chance to build a company all over again." He threw himself into it, working closely with the executives he had appointed to carry out the idea.

Perhaps inspired by how much he enjoyed starting Sam's, he was now also experimenting with several dot Discount Drug stores, a deep-discount pharmacy, and testing a new concept, Helen's Arts and Crafts. He was also entranced by the mall-sized hypermarkets he had seen on travels to scout retailing trends in Europe and Latin America. These giant marts combined huge grocery areas with Wal-Mart-like stores all under one roof. An Americanized Wal-Mart version would soon be in the works.

To keep Wal-Mart growing, several new distribution centers were under construction, which would allow the chain to continue to restock its store shelves much faster than the competition. To improve communication between Bentonville and stores that were farther and farther away, Wal-Mart was spending millions of dollars to install a satellite system that would allow Sam to send video messages to stores, speed up credit-card transactions, and let the company track sales almost as they happened.

Amid all that, Governor Bill Clinton called one day to ask a favor that would launch one of Sam's most creative—and controversial—crusades. Farris Fashions, a factory in Brinkley, Arkansas, had been making shirts for Penney and Sears under the Van Heusen brand name. But Van Heusen was moving its production to China, where wages were much lower. Ninety Arkansas jobs were on the line. Could Wal-Mart help?

After Sam and his executives weighed the idea, they decided to give it a try. "We're going to see if we can do something that's never been done before," Sam said.

Wal-Mart agreed to buy cloth—ironically, from Asia—so that Farris could make the flannel shirts in Arkansas. The workers kept their jobs, and the factory eventually would employ more than three hundred people. The agreement inspired Sam to try to see if he could expand that experience—and benefit from it.

In the mid-1980s, imports were getting plenty of attention. Japanese carmakers and their reliable, fuel-efficient models were gobbling up market share at the expense of U.S. automakers. All kinds of factories were closing in the U.S. and moving to countries where wages were lower.

Then–Arkansas governor Bill Clinton borrows a saxophone for an impromptu duet at a Wal-Mart store opening in 1990.

In a letter to three thousand Wal-Mart suppliers, Sam offered to work closely with them to keep or bring back U.S. jobs and to stem the increasing flow of imported goods from Asia, Latin America, and the Caribbean.

In 1986, he put together a major press conference, inviting manufacturers and politicians, and he challenged other retailers to join his "Bring It Home to the U.S.A." campaign. In front of a crowd from newspapers, magazines, and television, he held up a wire patio chair and boasted that Wal-Mart used to buy such chairs in bulk from China for $4.98 each. Now, he said, the chairs were coming from a plant in Indiana, and Wal-Mart was paying $3.50 each. He showed off washcloths, cooking utensils, windshield wipers, and candles that he was now buying from the United States. Even his shoes—which cost $29.48 at retail—came from Arkansas. He bragged that he was selling beach towels from maker J. P. Stevens for two for $7.00.

"If he doesn't sell these by sometime in the middle of summer, he is going to be up to his you-know-where in beach towels," joked Whitney Stevens, chairman of the towel company. That prompted Sam to wrap one of the towels around his waist. "We will sell them," he said confidently, even if it meant encouraging associates to wear them.

The salesmanship didn't stop with the big press conference. In stores, Wal-Mart hung "Made in the U.S.A." banners, posted tallies of how many thousands of jobs it had saved, and marked racks with signs that read, "This item, formerly imported, is now being purchased by Wal-Mart in the U.S.A." On television, it ran touching ads about how it had worked with bicycle and shirt factories to save

Sam holds up a lawn chair as an example of a product that had been made overseas but that became part of the 1986 kickoff to his Buy American campaign.

American jobs. Politicians publicly applauded the company for keeping jobs in their districts.

Shoppers were impressed, and some came to see the company as a champion of American workers. But almost no other retailers publicly joined Sam in his mission—because, in truth, both Wal-Mart and its competitors were also major buyers of products from overseas.

Wal-Mart had opened its first buying office in Hong Kong back in 1981. Because it was so determined to keep its prices low, the company was importing far more goods from Asia and elsewhere than its competitors. It relentlessly pressured suppliers to keep their prices low. That prompted many manufacturers to look at moving their own production overseas—just as Van Heusen had done with the flannel shirts that Farris made.

Sam realized there were also costs to all those imports. Foreign plants needed extra time to make and ship products, so Wal-Mart had to order imports months ahead, pay transportation costs, and maybe store the items in a warehouse for a while. Even then, the quality wasn't always very good. By contrast, U.S.-made goods could be made more quickly and could be delivered closer to when they would be needed.

In addition, those workers who were losing their factory jobs might well be Wal-Mart customers. Henry Ford, the famous carmaker, recognized in the early twentieth century that his workers needed decent paychecks to be able to buy Ford automobiles, so he raised their pay. "Wal-Mart is saying that if you don't buy the workers' goods, they're not going to be able to buy your goods," said a New York economic consultant. "It's all in Wal-Mart's enlightened self-interest."

Still, while Sam was willing to be more accommodating to U.S. factories, he wasn't willing to buy American-made goods unless the price was at least as cheap as buying from overseas. One U.S. clothing maker complained that it had lost a contract for 200,000 pairs of pants because Wal-Mart could buy them for 50 cents a pair less from a Caribbean manufacturer. But U.S. suppliers wouldn't complain publicly about losing contracts to foreign factories because Wal-Mart was such a large and powerful customer.

So even while Wal-Mart brought some jobs back to the United

States, the company was almost certainly increasing its imports every year as Wal-Mart grew. Some suppliers and competitors privately grumbled that the whole Made in the U.S.A. campaign was mainly about marketing. Sam didn't deny that Wal-Mart continued to import a lot of products—though neither he nor Wal-Mart would ever detail how much.

The program, which lasted for several years, was quintessential Sam Walton: He deeply believed in the mission, and his people invested significant time and effort in working with factories. At the same time, there wasn't a shred of charity involved. Wal-Mart benefited in many ways—in price, in quality, and from the warm customer response to Buy American. Was it real? Was it mostly for show? Ultimately, it was both.

After so many years of operating from little Bentonville, Sam wasn't used to the new scrutiny that accompanied Wal-Mart's growing clout and his own wealth. In addition to skepticism about the Buy American program, Wal-Mart was facing more and more criticism. People inside and outside the company wanted to see more women and minorities promoted, and small town merchants were starting to speak out about the way Wal-Mart romped over them when it came to town.

Female store managers at Wal-Mart were rare. Early on, Sam and other company officials assumed women wouldn't hop from store to store on a moment's notice, as Wal-Mart required managers to do. They also assumed women couldn't handle the physical labor of unloading or stocking merchandise. Even by the mid-1980s, Wal-Mart had few women buyers and no women or minorities at the rank of vice president or above. Management meetings often included special programs for wives—assuming that all the spouses were women.

There were no women or minorities on the board of directors, which oversaw the company on behalf of shareholders. Because Sam was the largest and most influential shareholder, that group was mostly made up of Sam's longtime friends and former retail executives. (One director, Charles Lazarus, the head of Toys "R" Us, was essentially a competitor, but Sam wanted him on the board to help Wal-Mart learn more about selling toys, a category Wal-Mart would eventually dominate.)

Though at least a couple of board members and executives, as well as Helen and Alice, had been pushing for a woman director, Sam resisted for years. In his generation, women rarely worked, and almost never led companies. Finally, in 1986, Hillary Rodham Clinton, the wife of Arkansas's governor, Bill Clinton, and a lawyer at a prominent Little Rock law firm, was elected to Wal-Mart's board. Clinton, in particular, pushed Sam to give women more opportunities, and by 1989, there were two woman vice presidents out of eighty-eight. But progress would be glacial.

For the first time since he opened a store in Rogers, Sam also began to see residents balk at the idea of a Wal-Mart coming to their communities. In Steamboat Springs, Colorado, beginning in 1986, residents fought off a Wal-Mart store for several years, arguing that a giant store on the edge of the mountain-resort community would hurt stores run by local residents and destroy a thriving downtown. In Iowa and Louisiana, townspeople also protested the stores.

Decades before, new suburban communities on the edges of cities had attracted shopping centers and malls, drawing consumers away from downtown stores and leaving central cities with empty storefronts. Now the pattern was repeating in smaller cities and towns as Wal-Mart and others built giant outlets on the highways, away from town centers. In a small place, where the downtown merchant might also be your neighbor, this shift felt more personal.

For instance, the 1983 arrival of a Wal-Mart in Pawhuska, Oklahoma, just as oil and farming businesses went into a slump, profoundly changed the town of 4,200. By 1987, a whole block of downtown stores had closed, including the J. C. Penney, the five-and-dime, and a television store. The Western Auto turned into an antiques store.

Bonnie Peters said her Peters Hardware was dropping the Corning and Oneida lines that Wal-Mart carried to focus on fancier gifts and bridal registries. "Wal-Mart didn't cause the trouble, but they haven't helped any," she said.

Wal-Mart managers were encouraged to be involved in the local community, but they didn't spend much. Local merchants were much more likely to buy ads in high school yearbooks and support Future Farmer pig sales. When Wal-Mart's manager didn't attend the Chamber of Commerce banquet, the Pawhuska newspaper called the chain "a billion-dollar parasite" and a "national retail ogre" for its skimpy financial contributions.

Worse for the local merchants, their longtime customers didn't understand why Wal-Mart's prices were so much lower. "People come in and say we're robbing them," said Fannie Berkenbile, who with her husband had run local pharmacies for forty years. "Some of my better customers were coming in here and waving the [Wal-Mart] ad in my face," said John E. Snider, a drugstore owner in Hominy, south of Pawhuska. "It hurt me professionally."

The pharmacists fought back with a lawsuit asking the state to enforce a 1941 law that required retailers to sell goods for a certain amount above their wholesale cost. Wal-Mart wanted the flexibility to charge less than that to bring customers in. It spent tens of thousands of dollars trying to get the law changed and challenging the suit. But it eventually lost and had to raise its prices.

Clearly the tables had turned. Sam Walton, who had started out much like the Berkenbiles, Bonnie Peters, and John Snider, with a store on the downtown square, was no longer the David in the battle against bigger retailers. Instead, in numerous newspaper and magazine stories, his chain was the Goliath that bullied and beat up on the little guys.

Sam didn't worry much about the fights over Wal-Mart's arrival, and he was truly baffled by the notion "that we are somehow the enemy of the small town." While competing merchants saw the chain as aggressive and ruthless in undercutting them, Sam saw Wal-Mart as providing the selection and low prices that shoppers wanted. To him, Wal-Mart was just practicing free enterprise and taking care of customers. He was certain that small stores would thrive if they offered services or items that Wal-Mart didn't have. And if they struggled, it wasn't Wal-Mart's doing. Rather, he argued, "the whole thing is driven by the customers, who are free to choose where to shop."

Fights over the opening of Wal-Mart stores became so common that Doonesbury creator Garry Trudeau ran a series of cartoons about them in the 1990s.

Truth be told, Sam was beginning to see the day when Wal-Mart might saturate small-town America and he wanted to find new ways to maintain his company's breakneck growth. In the fall of 1987, working with a Dallas grocery chain, he unveiled his first gargantuan Hypermart USA in the Dallas suburb of Garland, a store the size of almost five football fields, with a full grocery, tortilla bakery, seafood shop, fine jewelry department, tire and car-battery service, and gas station, and the kinds of prices that made Sam's Club successful. The "mall without walls" was intended to draw people from miles around, and more than fifty thousand people showed up the first week to see what the store looked like.

A week later, Wal-Mart opened a second Hypermart USA in Topeka, Kansas.

The company would get to just four Hypermarts, however, before deciding that the mammoth stores wouldn't earn enough profit to justify their size. But that experiment helped convince Wal-Mart that "supercenters," combination grocery and general stores, would fuel the next wave of its growth.

Before too long, Sam would give up on his dot Discount Drug store experiment and sell his four Helen's Arts and Crafts stores, deciding that neither of them fit in Wal-Mart's growth plans. Sam's Club was still expanding rapidly, and Wal-Mart was in only about half the states.

In early 1988, a couple of months before his seventieth birthday, Sam finally answered the succession question, naming Glass, the fifty-two-year-old president, as the chief executive officer. Shewmaker, the fifty-year-old financial chief, said he would retire to focus on cattle-breeding, though he would remain on Wal-Mart's board of directors. Sam continued to participate in Saturday morning meetings and remained deeply involved. After all, he and his family still owned about 40 percent of the company. But Glass would take over the day-to-day headaches.

The move freed Sam to do what he loved most: visiting stores, quizzing associates, and coming up with new ideas that might help blast discount rival Kmart and the nation's biggest retailer, Sears, from their lofty perches. One morning in late 1988, Sam, wearing a Wal-Mart baseball cap, went on the company's internal satellite system to share an idea to help boost sales during the holiday season.

"I don't think any other retail company in the world could do what

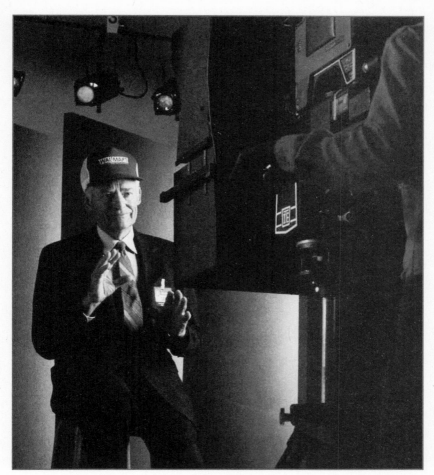

Sam passes along advice and encouragement to store employees in 1988 via the company's satellite system.

I'm going to propose to you," he said, warming up to his pitch. "It's simple. It won't cost us anything. And I believe it would just work magic, absolute magic, on our customers, and our sales would escalate, and I think we'd just shoot past our Kmart friends in a year or two and probably Sears as well."

All clerks had to do was look customers in the eye, greet them, and ask to help them. Even if you were shy or felt uncomfortable,

Sam said, he wanted you to learn to welcome a guest. "It would, I'm sure, help you become a leader, it would help your personality develop, you would become more outgoing," he promised. "It will do wonders for you."

Then, to seal the deal, he asked associates to raise their right hands and pledge to enforce what was known as Sam's "ten-foot rule": "From this day forward, I solemnly promise and declare that every customer that comes within ten feet of me, I will smile, look them in the eye, and greet them, so help me Sam."

Sam may have developed the idea from his college days, when he realized that the best way to win friends and fans was to greet people by name as he walked across campus. Management gurus would cite his ten-foot rule as effective customer service.

Wal-Mart was on a roll. The change in Wal-Mart's leadership hardly caused a hiccup. By early 1989, Wal-Mart had more than 1,250 discount stores, more than one hundred Sam's Clubs, and more than 200,000 employees. Its cash registers rang up $20.6 billion a year in sales—more than it had brought in during its first twenty-two years *combined*. In the last year of the decade, its sales would shoot up again, to $25.8 billion. And while it had started the eighties with $1 billion in sales, it would end this decade with $1 billion in profit. In 1987, it had been half the size of Kmart; in 1989, just two years later, the industry was abuzz with the possibility that Wal-Mart could pass Kmart in the next year or two.

The stock price was also climbing. In mid-1987, Wal-Mart's stock split for the eighth time—and for the fifth time in the 1980s.

A person who had 100 shares in 1970 would now have 25,600 shares worth more than $850,000. Sam's family worth had ballooned to as much as $8 billion—enough to spend $1 million every day for more than twenty years.

While he claimed to hate the attention and reluctantly signed the dollar bills that autograph seekers handed him, he didn't mind terribly that when he went into his stores, he was a bona fide celebrity with associates and customers. When he got on the microphone, people excitedly gathered around and hung on his every word.

But the wealth itself still didn't move him. In October 1987, the stock market swooned. The Dow Jones Industrial Average, an index that represents the broad stock market, lost more than 20 percent of its value in one day of wild, frantic trading. Wal-Mart's stock, which had been trading above $35 a share, plummeted to about $22. Within hours, Sam's fortune slid to less than $5 billion.

Reached that afternoon, he said he was concerned for his stockholders. But he shrugged off his own tremendous losses. "It's paper anyway," he said. "It was paper when we started, and it's paper afterward."

Perhaps. But with the 1980s ending and Sam in his eighth decade, investors, customers, and associates had to wonder what might happen to both Wal-Mart and that enormous, world-changing paper wealth without their patriarch and leader.

Chapter 10:

Big, Bigger, Biggest!

IN LATE 1989, Sam began to feel unusual aches and pains. On a hunting trip, he bruised his chest, and rather than healing, pain spread to his arm and got worse. Finally, he returned to his doctor in Houston.

He had faithfully visited Houston since he was diagnosed with leukemia in 1982, and a recent checkup had showed some small changes that his doctor wanted to investigate further. But Sam hadn't wanted to stick around for more tests.

At this appointment, however, the news was far more serious: Sam had multiple myeloma, a painful cancer of the bone marrow that was already softening his bones. Radiation and chemotherapy would slow down the disease and make him feel exhausted. But there was no cure.

Always private about his deepest feelings, Sam remained upbeat publicly. In early January 1990, he wrote associates about his new diagnosis, but not before first applauding Wal-Mart's successes—which included being named Retailer of the Decade by an industry magazine—and outlining goals for the new year. He tried to downplay the serious nature of his cancer, saying it was "really no big deal." He said he would spend a few weeks undergoing treatment and then looked forward to visiting stores again.

This time, Wal-Mart made the news public. It also made a point of noting that David Glass was now capably running the company and Sam had spent much of the crucial holiday season (as he often did) hunting birds. In a message in the February/March *Wal-Mart World*, Sam told associates that he was planning on attending a Saturday morning meeting on his return to Bentonville and had visited stores in the Houston area when he had felt up to it. Given that he had a great hunting season and the company was about to report another year of record sales and profits, he wrote, "I couldn't be more blessed." He reminded colleagues to "continue to listen to those wonderful customers of ours and take care of their needs as they shop with us." And he urged each of them to become "the very best person we possibly can be."

With mortality staring him in the face, Sam reflected on his remaining years. Now nearly seventy-two years old, should he withdraw from the company altogether to spend time with Helen, his children, and his grandchildren? Should he devote his energy to making a substantial and life-changing contribution to a cause with that enormous fortune in Wal-Mart stock?

He tried on the possibilities. But none of them really fit.

To Sam's relief, he had moved down from the top spot on the

Forbes' "richest Americans" list after the magazine began to recognize that their four children shared equally in the company with Sam and Helen. These days, the magazine divided the family fortune, now estimated at more than $20 billion, among Sam and his children. While they each still ranked third, behind media magnate John W. Kluge and just below Microsoft founder Bill Gates, Sam happily wasn't getting as much attention. Even after decades of significant wealth, Sam had never been especially comfortable either with his prosperity or with giving money away.

Wal-Mart itself was stingy, by design. Through a nonprofit foundation established in the early 1980s, each store gave a $1,000 scholarship to a local student, a tiny fraction of what it took in from the community. Employees who raised money for a local cause could request a matching grant from the foundation. It also donated to local United Ways, which support community organizations, in a relationship dating back to 1983. But, Sam said, "We feel very strongly that Wal-Mart really is *not*, and *should not* be, in the charity business."

Rather, its first and main goal was to give customers low prices, which he saw as its own way of giving back to the community. "We don't believe in taking a lot of money out of Wal-Mart's cash registers and giving it to charity," he said—even when Wal-Mart was singled out for its lower-than-average giving—because the money has to come from either customers or shareholders. The average company donated a little more than 1 percent of pretax profit to charity. Wal-Mart gave less than half of that, while Kmart gave more than 1 percent of pretax earnings and Target was unusually charitable, giving about 5 percent of pretax profit.

Sam and Helen were more generous personally. They donated $6 million to the Presbyterian Church, started a program that allowed students from Central America to study at Arkansas colleges, and supported an organization called Students in Free Enterprise, which encouraged college students to learn about the value of business and entrepreneurship. Education was a major focus of their philanthropy, and they gave to several local universities. In Bentonville, they donated funds to, among other things, upgrade the public library, build a recreation center, and support a fine-arts center.

They also personally built a fitness facility in Bentonville for Wal-Mart employees. (Such a health club was sorely needed. Years of heavy travel and six-day weeks took a toll on Wal-Mart managers and executives. David Glass suffered a heart attack in the mid-1980s, as did a senior financial officer. Others had open-heart surgery. An early employee who retired in the 1980s said the extensive dental work he needed after his retirement grew out years of bad eating and stress related to the intense work and days on the road.)

The interest in charitable giving came not from Sam but from

Sam and Helen in the late 1980s. They focused much of their giving on education, the Presbyterian church, and Arkansas needs.

Helen, who told others, "It isn't what you gather in life, it's what you share that tells the kind of life you have lived." She wasn't alone in pushing Sam to give. Ewing Kauffman, a wealthy Kansas City philanthropist, encouraged Sam to share some of his riches, telling him that giving away money had been more fun than making it. But Sam just wasn't bent that way. Nor could he bring himself to retire. Helen certainly would have liked him to slow down and hang around the house more. In fact, during his cancer treatment, she was spending more time with him than ever, and she enjoyed it. "The lifestyle changes have been wonderful for me," she told a reporter that April. "Sam and I hardly saw each other up until he got sick."

During the nights when he couldn't sleep, Sam wrestled with the deeper questions about his life, which for decades had focused almost entirely on his work. "Was it really worth all the time I spent away from my family? Should I have driven my partners so hard all those years? Am I really leaving behind something on this earth that I can be proud of having accomplished, or does it somehow lack meaning to me now that I'm facing the ultimate challenge?" he asked himself. "In the larger sense—the life and death sense—did I make the right choices?"

Ultimately, he decided, he had. "If I wanted to reach the goals I set for myself, I had to get at it and stay at it every day. I had to think about it all the time," he wrote in his autobiography—and that's essentially what he had done. Others might argue that Wal-Mart had been too tough on small-town merchants, pushed manufacturers too hard for lower prices, or worked its people to the bone, but Sam was absolutely sure that he had made life better for many

Americans. "We've improved the standard of living of our customers, whom we've saved billions of dollars, and of our associates, who have been able to share profits," he said. "I believe that millions of people are better off today than they would have been if Wal-Mart had never existed."

Given that, he concluded, "I can honestly say that if I had the choices to make all over again, I would make just about the same ones. . . . I am just awfully proud of the whole deal, and I feel good about how I chose to expend my energies in this life."

The soul-searching led to a meaningful revelation: If Sam had only a limited time left, he ought to spend it on what mattered most to him—and that was Wal-Mart.

At Wal-Mart's annual meeting of shareholders in June 1990, Sam pumped up the gathering as never before. In front of more than eight thousand shareholders and employees at the University of Arkansas sports arena, he once again challenged them to meet an audacious goal. Noting that Wal-Mart had rung up nearly $26 billion in sales for the year ending in early 1990, he told the crowd that he was sure the company could do five times that business by 2000—nearly *$130 billion*. Though Wal-Mart now had more than 1,400 stores, he believed that number could double, as could the number of Sam's Clubs. After all, it was in only twenty-seven states at the moment; it had just dipped a toe in Minnesota and Michigan and hadn't yet reached California. It expected to open stores in seven new states in the next year.

"I really believe it's possible," Sam said. And then he shouted, "Can we do it?"

"Yes we can!" the crowd roared back.

The stock—which made Sam wealthy and bulked up profit-sharing accounts for workers, with contributions equaling about 6 percent of their annual pay—jumped $2 that day, to close at $58 a share. Before the month was over, Wal-Mart's stock would climb to more than $60 a share, and it would split again, for the ninth time. Any lucky person who had purchased 100 shares in 1970 for $1,650 and simply held on as Wal-Mart conquered town after town, state after state, would now own more than 51,000 shares worth more than $1.5 million, a stunning gain in twenty years.

Some six months later, Wal-Mart accomplished another seemingly impossible feat: It squeaked past both Kmart and Sears to become America's largest retailer. In the year that ended in early 1991, it recorded $32.6 billion in sales, ahead of Kmart's $32.1 billion and Sears' $32 billion. And it did it with the same kinds of sales that had helped launch Sam back in Newport and Bentonville: underwear and socks. In 1991, Wal-Mart would sell 135 million men's and boys' briefs, 136 million women's panties, and 280 million pairs of socks, enough to outfit everyone in America.

But Sam, always looking for ways to make his company better, still wasn't satisfied. When he felt up to it, he was back flying his plane, his plastic SAM ID badge on his jacket, visiting stores. As always, there were no personal assistants or drivers—just Wal-Mart's founder and largest owner ready to inspect shelves, floors, prices, and the performance of each department.

At 7 a.m. one morning, he toured a store in Memphis, Tennessee,

Sam ended every store visit by leading a rousing version of the Wal-Mart cheer, as he does here at a Hypermart opening in the late 1980s.

making note of a baby oil display and congratulating a manager named Renee for running one of the ten best pet departments in the company. Then, picking up the store microphone, he called employees up front and started with a compliment: "The company is so proud of you, we can't hardly stand it."

Still, he told them, there was more work to do. "That confounded Kmart is getting better, and so is Target," he warned. So, he asked, "Are you thinking about doing those extra little things? Are you lookin' the customer in the eye and offering to help?"

The store sales were up, he told them, but then asked if they could do a little better. "We've got to continue to improve," he urged, before finishing with the Wal-Mart cheer.

Over four days of visiting stores, he would lunch with associates in Savannah, Tennessee; check out milk prices at the Kroger in Batesville, Arkansas; reminisce with longtime employees in Conway, Arkansas; and help open a Sam's Club in Marion, Illinois. It was, wrote *Fortune* writer John Huey, who accompanied him on this trip, an ongoing "farewell tour of Sam Walton, America's undisputed merchant king of the late 20th century."

With the cancer advancing, however, Sam's trips would wind down by the end of 1991. He was growing too weak to continue them. There was, though, one piece of unfinished business. At the persistent urging of family and co-workers, he agreed to finish his memoirs, which he had started in 1988 and then dropped. He hired Huey as his writer, and received a $4 million advance from publisher Doubleday, unheard for a book by a businessman, pledging his earnings to support new approaches to education.

The deadline was tight. But Sam was focused, working on the project daily, with the same attention he applied to store visits.

He also wrote a final column in *Wal-Mart World*, both applauding employees and pushing them to do more. "Together, we can do anything, even to being the best as well as the largest retailer in the world," he wrote. "Good luck, partners, for 1992 and beyond. You're great, and again, I appreciate your affection, love, friendship, and all that you've done to make Wal-Mart and SAM's number one. Best, always.

"Your partner and friend, Sam Walton"

An ailing Sam waves to employees in March 1992 after President George H. W. Bush presented him with the Medal of Freedom.

After receiving just about every retailing and business recognition imaginable and gracing the covers of numerous magazines, there seemed little left to accomplish. But in early March 1992, the White House called. President George H. W. Bush wanted to fly to Bentonville—the territory of Bill Clinton, whom he would face in the November election—to award Sam the Medal of Freedom, one of the nation's highest civilian awards.

On March 17, before many associates in the Wal-Mart auditorium, President Bush and First Lady Barbara Bush recognized an ailing Sam, who was so weak that he had to be rolled out in a wheelchair. The president recounted Sam's modest start, his daring flying and poor driving, his commitment to his associates, and his iron-willed ambition. He noted that with 380,000 employees, more people worked for Wal-Mart than lived in Tulsa, Oklahoma. This award wasn't about money or philanthropy. "It's about determination. It's about leadership," he said. "The story of Sam Walton is an illustration of the American dream."

When the time came to present the medal, Sam insisted on standing, to huge applause, though it was obviously difficult and he had to steady himself with the wheelchair. The citation read, in part, "A devoted family man, business leader, and statesman for democracy, Sam Walton demonstrates the virtues of faith, hope, and hard work. America honors this captain of commerce, as successful in life as in business." When President Bush put the medal around his neck, the room erupted in a long, thundering ovation.

It would be his last public appearance, his last Wal-Mart meeting. A few days later, Sam was admitted to the hospital. On April 5, 1992, about a week after his seventy-fourth birthday, Sam Walton died.

He was buried in a private funeral. A company memorial service closed to the press drew more than 1,500 Wal-Mart employees and was broadcast to all the Wal-Mart stores via the company's satellite system. A public service that night at a Bentonville football field drew another thousand friends and admirers.

Mr. Sam, the ambitious, driven, energetic, and charismatic leader, was gone. But his creation was very much alive. His high-flying, thriving Wal-Mart stores had yet to reach all fifty states. His expanding family fortune rivaled any America had ever seen. Sam's work was far from finished.

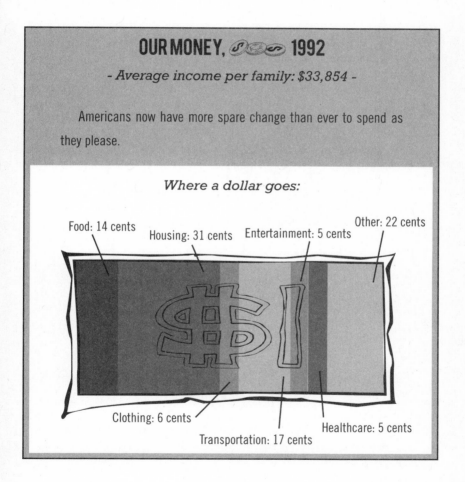

OUR MONEY, 1992

- Average income per family: $33,854 -

Americans now have more spare change than ever to spend as they please.

Where a dollar goes:

Food: 14 cents
Housing: 31 cents
Entertainment: 5 cents
Other: 22 cents
Clothing: 6 cents
Transportation: 17 cents
Healthcare: 5 cents

HISTORY OF LOGOS

WALMART   1962–1964

WAL·MART   1964–1981

   1968–1981

WAL-MART   1981–1992

WAL★MART°   1992–2008

   2008–present

Epilogue

IN WAYS BIG and small, Wal-Mart was a different company without Sam Walton.

David Glass continued as the chief executive officer until 2000, and Sam's oldest son, Rob, became the company's new chairman. While Rob knew the company inside and out, he didn't have his dad's charisma or the same relationship with associates.

Wal-Mart continued to grow, though it didn't expand as quickly as before. While its longtime competitor Kmart struggled, Wal-Mart easily met Sam's 1990 challenge of $130 billion in annual sales by the turn of the century—a year early. By the end of January 2000, its annual sales reached $165 billion, and it was doing business in all fifty United States as well as Canada, Mexico, Britain, Germany, Argentina, and Brazil.

In the decade that followed, it more than doubled in size again, reaching $405 billion in annual sales in the fiscal year that ended in January 2010, making it the world's largest company. It is more than four times the size of the next largest retailer, CVS Caremark, and more than five times the size of either Kroger or Target.

Rob, Sam's oldest son, remains chairman of Wal-Mart, carrying on the family legacy.

Still, the issues that originally flared up before Sam's death—whether Wal-Mart really brought manufacturing back to the U.S.A., whether it was doing enough to promote women and minorities, and how Wal-Mart affected communities when it came to town—continued to fester as the company grew larger and moved up the East and West Coasts. Increasingly, it came under fire on several fronts:

Starting with a little-noticed press release in 1991, the year before Sam died, and escalating into the middle 1990s, unions, human-rights activists, and the media accused Wal-Mart of buying from factories in Asia and Latin America that employed young children and abused employees, working them too many hours or paying them too little. Some of the allegations grew out of investigations into the company's Buy American campaign.

The company initially denied some of the accusations and said it had resolved others by dropping some manufacturers. But under pressure from critics, the media, and a large shareholder, Wal-Mart agreed to adopt a formal code of conduct for the factories that made its goods and to monitor manufacturers. Other retailers soon followed suit.

But the code wasn't well enforced. In 1996, a labor activist disclosed that children were working long days for pennies an hour making garments sold under the Kathie Lee Gifford brand at Wal-Mart. The media attention that followed pushed Wal-Mart to more aggressively keep an eye on its manufacturers. Still, poor working conditions and child labor at the roughly 100,000 suppliers of items sold at Wal-Mart stores remain a concern.

Today, Wal-Mart publishes an annual Global Sustainability Report that details, among other things, the results of thousands of factory inspections, which continue to uncover health and safety issues, failure to pay wages and overtime, and other problems. By the company's own account, the majority of its suppliers worldwide are cited each year for violations of its code of conduct.

Particularly in the last decade, the company has faced an increasing number of lawsuits and accusations related to how it treats its employees. Perhaps reflecting Sam's early unwillingness to promote women, in 2001, six current and former female employees sued Wal-Mart, charging that it denied them the same pay and promotion opportunities given to men. Courts have ruled that the lawsuit, which was still pending in 2010, can move forward on behalf of more than one million current and former female employees.

In 2004, a *New York Times* story disclosed that workers at a small number of stores were locked in overnight as they restocked shelves. Some employees who suffered medical emergencies had to wait for a manager to arrive with a key before they could leave the store. The company said it discontinued lock-ins after they became public, but just the thought that such a practice could exist tarnished the company's image.

In addition, in dozens of lawsuits, workers sued the company for forcing them to work without pay after their shifts ended or denying them lunch and other breaks. In 2008, the company settled many of them, agreeing to pay at least $350 million to employees.

As Wal-Mart began to blanket the U.S. and reach up into New England in the 1990s, it became embroiled in more and more fights with future neighbors and store opponents, who argued that a store's arrival would kill local businesses and close the downtown area while bringing in traffic and outsiders. Academic studies found that its presence did, indeed, hurt existing groceries, drugstores, toy stores, and other retailers who competed directly with it, and that overall, it didn't add many new jobs after the jobs lost at other stores were factored in.

At the same time, a new Wal-Mart in town helped other business, like restaurants or specialty stores. And, not surprisingly, it brought lower prices to communities. That especially helped lower-income families, the backbone of Wal-Mart's customer base. More than 55 percent of the chain's customers today have annual household income of less than $50,000 a year, a budget tight enough that saving money on toilet paper, toothpaste, and groceries really matters.

Did Wal-Mart lose its way after Sam died? Some people believe it did. They see the company as a greedy, cheap, demanding, and even evil monster that devours workers, competitors, and manufacturers who are just trying to make a decent living. Others think that Sam's legacy lives. They laud Wal-Mart's efficiency, discipline, and low prices, and regularly vote the company to *Fortune* magazine's list of America's "most admired" companies.

Charles Fishman, who wrote a bestselling book, *The Wal-Mart Effect*, which detailed how the powerful chain affects suppliers, communities, and employees, came down somewhere in the middle. Wal-Mart didn't lose the culture that Sam instilled; the company is still frugal, driven, modest, and unpretentious, he writes. Rather, "Wal-Mart has literally outgrown those values." When Sam and Wal-Mart were little upstarts bringing lower prices to small communities in the South, they were much like a ten-year-old big brother wrestling with a younger sibling. But when that kid grows to be the size of a National Football League lineman, the horseplay is something completely different. As Wal-Mart grew to a breathtaking size, its relentless focus on low prices first—perhaps at the cost of factory workers, suppliers, communities, and its own associates—has had a completely different, and sometimes unexpected, impact.

Nearly two decades after Sam's death, fewer and fewer people remember Sam or Bud, who passed away in 1995. The second generation is beginning to think about the role of the third generation. Both Rob, the oldest son, and Jim, the third son, sit on Wal-Mart's board of directors, as does Gregory Penner, Rob's forty-year-old son-in-law.

John, the second son, who had directed the family's philanthropy, died in 2005 at the age of fifty-eight when a plane he was flying crashed shortly after takeoff in Wyoming. He left behind a wife and son.

Helen died of natural causes in 2007 at the age of eighty-seven, and was remembered for her role in helping shape the company's direction and employee benefits. In her later years, she increased the family's giving, donating $300 million to the University of Arkansas and another $50 million to its business school.

Though Sam may have built the company with a tight fist, Helen, with her generosity, might well have the last word. Helen and Sam together owned one-fifth of Walton Enterprises, the family partnership, and their share will go to charity over a number of years. The family has said that some of its Wal-Mart stock will have to be sold to fund her bequests.

In 2010, Walton Enterprises owned 1.68 billion Wal-Mart shares, or about 40 percent of the company, valued at roughly $90 billion. Along with other investments, the combined value of the Walton family's fortune exceeded $100 billion—an eye-popping sum that is more than the combined wealth of America's richest man, Microsoft founder Bill Gates, and the second-richest, super-investor Warren

The Walton family remains a large owner in Wal-Mart Stores. Above, Helen joins sons Rob, left, and John at the 2001 company annual meeting. Below, Rob, Alice, and Jim take the stage at the 2009 meeting.

Buffett. In addition, the family receives almost $2 billion a year in cash dividends.

That kind of fortune—enough to spend $10 million every single day for more than twenty-five years—could create a charitable legacy as great as any the world has ever seen. But two things have to happen: The Walton family must want to do it, and Wal-Mart must continue to thrive and grow.

Rob, Jim, and Alice, now in their sixties, have said in the past that they are still focused mainly on building Wal-Mart, not on giving their money away. Alice, however, has invested both time and family money in an ambitious art museum, Crystal Bridges, in Bentonville.

Helped along by additional contributions from Helen's estate, the Walton Family Foundation had more than $2 billion in holdings at the end of 2009, sizeable among charitable foundations, but just a tiny fraction of the family's riches. With an emphasis on school choice and charter schools, conservation, and northwest Arkansas, it gave away about $378 million in 2009. The year before his death, John told a reporter that he expected the family's charitable interests to broaden and the amount of giving to grow over time—but he wasn't clear if that meant years, decades, or generations.

There is no guarantee, however, that wealth so tied up in a single company will hold its value. Wal-Mart hasn't had a stock split since 1999, and its share price has traded between about $42 and $65 a share for a decade. As Sam knew, stock "is only paper" and that paper value can soar or plunge in a heartbeat.

It may seem inconceivable now that Wal-Mart could ever lose its place as the world's dominant retailer. But no company in any industry stays in the top spot forever. Not General Motors. Not Sears, Roebuck, the most powerful retailer for much of the twentieth century, or Kmart, the leading discounter. In fact, Kmart reorganized under bankruptcy laws in 2002, and it merged with Sears, Roebuck in 2005. Together, they aren't among the ten biggest American retailers today.

Even Sam recognized that success can be fleeting, writing in his autobiography, "There's always a challenger coming along. There may be one on the street right now formulating a plan to get to the

Even after Sam's death, Wal-Mart continued to grow, while Kmart and Sears struggled, eventually merging into one company.

top." Wal-Mart, he said, "is just another chapter in that history of competition—a great chapter, mind you—but it's all part of the evolution of the industry."

What could challenge Wal-Mart? It could be another store chain, or it could be an online retailer like Amazon.com, which doesn't need sprawling stores, vast parking lots, or even smiling clerks and greeters to provide shoppers access to millions of well-priced items. Amazon.com right now is just a minnow to Wal-Mart's whale; in fact, Wal-Mart rings up the equivalent of Amazon's annual sales every few weeks. But then, Wal-Mart was once just a fraction of the size of Sears and Kmart.

Of course, the next Wal-Mart may not be Amazon.com or any other company we know today. It may just be in the future of an ambitious, determined, and competitive kid growing up right now, someone with a dream, a single-minded focus, and a willingness to work very hard. You never know.

OUR MONEY, 2008

- Average income per family: $63,563 -

The basics—food, housing, and clothing—now take about 51 cents of every dollar, down from 78 cents when Sam was born, leaving more money to spend on iPods, cell phones, and video games.

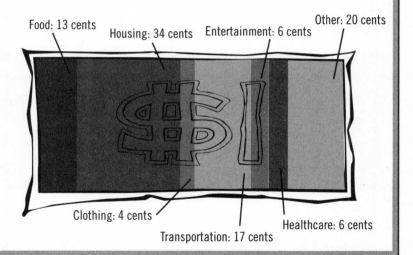

Where a dollar goes:

Food: 13 cents

Housing: 34 cents

Entertainment: 6 cents

Other: 20 cents

Clothing: 4 cents

Transportation: 17 cents

Healthcare: 6 cents

NOTES

For a journalist, Sam Walton was a tough executive to cover. He didn't like to be interviewed, and he didn't care much for the press. I wrote about Wal-Mart on and off over five years for the *Wall Street Journal* and he never granted me an interview, though I did see him in action a few times and once joined a store tour that he led for Wall Street analysts.

When Sam did talk to reporters, he was usually all business, and few stories capture much of a personal side. He occasionally opened up about personal travels, hunting, or Helen in his monthly column or other articles in the company newsletter, *Wal-Mart World*, but even those asides are brief. As a result, many of the quotations from Sam himself come from his auto-biography, a book that was mostly done in a hurry during Sam's last year of life. The next best authority on Sam's early life is Vance H. Trimble, author of *Sam Walton: The Inside Story of America's Richest Man*, who went back to Sam's early homes and haunts and interviewed old friends and acquaintances.

In addition to drawing on my own previous reporting, I dug up and read through dozens of articles about Sam, Wal-Mart, and its competitors in retailing publications, *Wal-Mart World*, national newspapers, and national magazines dating back to the 1960s, in microfilm of Arkansas papers at the Bentonville Public Library and the library of the University of Arkansas in Fayetteville, and in clipping files at the Shiloh Museum of Ozark History in Springdale and the Rogers Historical Museum. Flagler Productions in Kansas City, Missouri, opened up its collection and the Wal-Mart Visitor

Center in Bentonville had one-of-a-kind memorabilia. The personal papers of James Cash Penney and the JCPenney Archives at Southern Methodist University were also helpful. Journalists in Newport and Bentonville, Arkansas, were kind enough to consult their own clip files to assist with dates and facts. In addition, I sought interviews with Wall Street analysts who knew Sam well, Wal-Mart old-timers, Walton family members, and John Huey, the writer of Walton's autobiography and perhaps the reporter who knew him best. Early on, I asked Wal-Mart for interviews with a couple of executives and for access to archives and photographs. Both Wal-Mart and Walton family members declined my requests.

The notes below cite sources of quotations and occasionally elaborate on issues in the text where details may be in dispute.

INTRODUCTION

"We've got the best group . . .": McCord, "Stockholders on a Locker-Room High."

CHAPTER 1: WIN! WIN! WIN!

Eagle Scout: Sam says in his autobiography that he was thirteen when he became an Eagle Scout, but Boy Scouts of America records show that he was awarded the honor in March 1934, making him fifteen.

"It is a fact . . .": Walton, *Made in America*, 15.

"It was tragic . . .": Walton, *Made in America*, 5.

"I have always pursued everything . . .": Walton, *Made in America*, 15, 18.

"Mother and Dad were . . .": Walton, *Made in America*, 5.

"Sam did all right . . .": Trimble, *Sam Walton*, 29.

"Heavyset hyperthyroid...": "Hustler Walton," Beta Theta Pi fraternity article.

"I was tired . . .": Walton, *Made in America*, 22.

"I liked what . . .": Trimble, *Sam Walton*, 32–33.

Our Money: Dolfman and McSweeney. All of the "Our Money" graphics, except for 1945 and 2008, are drawn from this study.

Mr. Sam

CHAPTER 2: WAR!

"Does it square with . . .": Penney, *Fifty Years with the Golden Rule*, 104.

Major received a bonus check: Walton, *Made in America*, 23, says Major's check was for $65,000, but that amount seems highly unlikely, given Sam's salary of less than $1,000 a year. Plus, a $65,000 check in the early 1940s would be equivalent to about $1 million today.

"It was a seven-day . . ." and "Maybe you're just not . . .": Walton, *Made in America*, 23.

"I loved retail . . .": Walton, *Made in America*, 22.

"I want to show you . . ." and "Boys, you know . . .": Trimble, *Sam Walton*, 35.

"Haven't I met you . . .": Walton, *Made in America*, 24.

"I wanted to fly so bad . . .": "High Profile," *Arkansas Democrat*, 8.

"I thought life with him . . .": Cooper, "For Richer and Richer," *Ladies' Home Journal*.

Our Money, 1945: Current Population Reports, March 2, 1948.

HOW SYLVAN GOLDMAN MOVED THE WORLD

"it was a complete . . ." and "I have been . . .": Tedlow, *New and Improved*, 231.

PENNEY PINCHING

"From now on . . .": Penney, *Fifty Years with the Golden Rule*, 13.

"We threw away no . . .": Penney, *Fifty Years with the Golden Rule*, 57.

CHAPTER 3: SELL! SELL! SELL!

"a real dog . . .": Walton, *Made in America*, 28.

"I'd bring them back . . .": Walton, *Made in America*, 31.

"This is really . . .": Walton, *Made in America*, 33.

"I became accustomed . . .": "From Our Founders . . ." *Wal-Mart World*, 18.

"We had to keep expenses . . .": Walton, *Made in America*, 36.

"that's all I could . . .": "From Our Founders . . ." *Wal-Mart World*, 4.

"I figured I'd rather . . ." : Walton, *Made in America*, 36.

"I'm sure it . . .": Walton, *Made in America*, 29–30.

"I never forgave him . . .": Walton, *Made in America*, 36.

"It can't be . . .": Walton, *Made in America*, 37–38.

"It really was . . .": Walton, *Made in America*, 39.

CHAPTER 4: FLYING!

"big business deal": "Big Business Deal," *Benton County Democrat*, 1.

"Lovely" and "an exceptional value": "Announcing Our Remodeling Sale,"
    Walton's 5 & 10 advertisement in the *Benton County Democrat*.

"One thing . . . pretty ragged": Walton, *Made in America*, 43.

"an attractive addition . . .": "Grand Opening Thursday," *Benton County
    Democrat*, 1.

"Up and coming businessman": "Grand Opening Thursday," *Benton County
    Democrat*, 1.

"Don't get the idea . . .": Walton, *Made in America*, 88.

"Dad thrived . . .": Walton, *Made in America*, 90.

"Dad and I . . .": Walton, *Made in America*, 91.

"I probably could have . . .": Flagler Productions, video of visit to Old High
    Middle School.

"I made all . . . pretty good": Walton, *Made in America*, 96.

"This was . . .": Harris, author interview.

"The world's worst . . ." Walton, *Made in America*, 51.

"I figured anyone. . . .": "From Our Founders . . ." *Wal-Mart World*, 18.

"Do you have . . . talk to Brother": Reinboth, author interview.

"It turned out . . .": Walton, *Made in America*, 64.

SAM STORIES: THE MISTAKE

"going to sweep . . ." and "I was going . . .": From Our Founders . . ." *Wal-Mart
    World*, 3.

"I decided . . .": Walton, *Made in America*, 50.

CHAPTER 5: CHEAP! CHEAP! CHEAP!

Headlines quoted from *Time*; *BusinessWeek*; and *U.S. News & World Report*.

Mr. Sam

"The public thinks . . .": "Gibson's L'il Ole Billion-Dollar Business,"
   BusinessWeek.
"I wasn't about . . .": Walton, *Made in America*, 55.
"Our stores are . . .": "How Kresge Became the Top Discounter." *BusinessWeek*.
"We sell for less" and "Satisfaction guaranteed.": Walton, *Made in America*, 57.
"Dating often" and "Sam and Bud . . .": Helen Walton, "Seasons Greetings."
"Sam Walton, is . . . educational process": Walton, *Made in America*, 62.
"truly ugly": Walton, *Made in America*, 59.
"the worst retail store . . . and how we're doing": Huey, "Wal-Mart: Will It Take
   Over the World?" *Fortune*.
"After we got . . .": Walton, *Made in America*, 59.
"a certain motivation. . . .": Leveritt, "The Wal-Mart Way," *Arkansas Times*, 105.
"ESP": Walton, *Made in America*, 68.
"We're with Walton's . . . Next to Rogers": Walton, *Made in America*, 84

BLACK AND WHITE IN THE 1960S

"You Better Not" and "I realized . . .": Harris, author interview.
"first Negro entertainer": Duty, "Hinted Racial Trouble Absent."

CHAPTER 6: GOING PUBLIC!

"didn't want it . . .": Walton, *Made in America*, 127.
"Just one more store" and "When we . . .": "From Our Founders . . ." *Wal-Mart
   World*, 3.
"I couldn't get . . .": "High Profile," *Arkansas Democrat*, 8.
"I always felt . . .": Walton, *Made in America*, 127.
"It was the closest . . .": Trimble, *Sam Walton*, 4.
"Super-rich": McFadden, "America's New Super-Rich Men," *New York Times*.
"the biggest single. . . ." and "Because the way . . .": Walton, *Made in America*, 164.
"All of us like . . .": Walton, *Made in America*, 179.
"would praise us . . .": Ely, "Associate Spotlight," *Wal-Mart World*, 5.
"We make no bones . . .": "Small-Town Hit," *Time*.
"That's a pretty . . .": Trimble, *Sam Walton*, 138–39.
"I'll never forget . . .": Walton, *Made in America*, 210.
"I would hate . . ." and "it was one of": Loveless, author interview.

"Now, Helen . . ." and "Yes, Sam": Ortega, *In Sam We Trust*, 197.
"Saturday night massacre": Walton, *Made in America*, 195.
"I wasn't able . . .": "Wal-Mart Stores Chief Resigns," *Wall Street Journal*.
"The truth is . . .": Walton, *Made in America*, 192.
"For the first time . . . :" Walton, *Made in America*, 196.

SAM STORIES: AIR HEAD

"Oh, it's a big sky.": Mason, "Sam Walton of Wal-Mart," *BusinessWeek*, 142.

SAM STORIES: OUT OF THE TOILET

"Sam would be . . .": Leveritt, "The Wal-Mart Way," *Arkansas Times*, 116.

CHAPTER 7: GROW! GROW! GROW!

"Write it on the wall . . .": Reddish, "People of the Financial World," *Financial World*, 28–29.
"Meet them . . .": Walton, *Made in America*, 245.
"Magic circle": Wal-Mart Stores Inc. Annual Report for the year ended Jan. 31, 1972, 5.
"What do you . . . good as that one": Soderquist, *The Wal-Mart Way*, 20–21.
"I'm really impressed . . . eight or ten years": Seneker, "A Day in the Life of Sam Walton," *Forbes*, 45–48.
"What they had . . .": Walton, *Made in America*, 245
"Polyester palace": Ortega, *In Sam We Trust*, 120.
"Nothing can stop . . .": Carruth, "Kmart Has to Open Some New Doors," *Fortune*, 154.
"The best guess . . .": "Wal-Mart: A Discounter Sinks Deep Roots in Small Town, U.S.A., *BusinessWeek*.

SAM STORIES: BACK TO NEWPORT

"By then, I was . . ." "We did . . ." and "His customers . . .": Walton, *Made in America*, 225–26.

CHAPTER 8: RICH, RICHER, RICHEST!

"Then, he would make . . .": Walton, *Made in America*, 149.

"We've always . . .": Walton, "Message from Sam Walton," *Wal-Mart World*, 2.

"condition was . . .": Mason, "Sam Walton of Wal-Mart," *BusinessWeek*, 142.

"You'll never . . .": Garcia, "People," *Time*.

"It was one . . .": Walton, *Made in America*, 203.

"It was a . . .": Harris, "America's Richest Man," *Washington Post*.

"Early Bus Station": Mason, "Sam Walton of Wal-Mart," *BusinessWeek*, 142.

"It's not money . . .": Harris, "America's Richest Man," *Washington Post*.

"Maybe it's none . . .": Walton, *Made in America*, 218–19.

SAM STORIES: OL' ROY

"I just thoroughly . . .": Huey, "The Secret Life," *Southpoint*, 60.

"He had a reputation . . .": Ortega, *In Sam We Trust*, 189.

"Roy was probably . . .": Walton, *Made in America*, 187.

CHAPTER 9: GO! GO! GO!

"was almost what. . . .": Walton, *Made in America*, 257.

"We're going to see . . .": Barrier, "Walton's Mountain," *Nation's Business*, 21.

"If he doesn't sell . . .": Flagler Productions, transcript of manager's meeting,

"This item, formerly . . .": Ortega, *In Sam We Trust*, 208.

"Wal-Mart is saying . . .": Kilborn, "Wal-Mart's 'Buy American,'" *New York Times*.

"Wal-Mart didn't cause . . . It hurt me professionally . . .": Blumenthal, "Arrival of Discounter," *Wall Street Journal*, 1A.

"that we are somehow . . .": Walton, *Made in America*, 226.

"the whole thing . . .": Walton, *Made in America*, 228.

"mall without walls": Trimble, *Sam Walton*, 295.

"I don't think . . . so help me Sam": Huey, "Wal-Mart: Will It Take Over the World?," *Fortune*.

"It's paper . . .": Associated Press, "Walton: Loses Another $1 Billion-Plus."

Our Money, 1992: U.S. Bureau of Labor Statistics Consumer Expenditure Survey.

CHAPTER 10: BIG, BIGGER, BIGGEST!

"really no big deal": Ortega, *In Sam We Trust*, 218–19.

"I couldn't be . . .": Walton, "Message to Associates," February/March 1990,
    Wal-Mart World.

"We feel very . . ." and "We don't believe . . .": Walton, *Made in America*, 306.

"It isn't what you . . .": Flagler Productions, Helen Walton memorial video.

"The lifestyle changes . . .": "High Profile," *Arkansas Democrat*, 5.

"Was it really . . ." and "If I wanted to . . .": Walton, *Made in America*, 319–20.

"We've improved . . .": Walton, *Made in America*, 320–21.

"I believe that millions . . .": Walton, *Made in America*, 321–22.

"I can honestly say . . .": Walton, *Made in America*, 320.

"I am just awfully . . .": Walton, *Made in America*, 322.

"I really believe . . .": Tomsho, "Wal-Mart's Walton," *Wall Street Journal*.

"The company is so . . . continue to improve" and "farewell tour of . . .": Huey,
    "America's Most Successful Merchant," *Fortune*.

"Together, we can . . .": Walton, "Message to Associates: Our Focus for '92,"
    Wal-Mart World.

"It's about . . .": Bush, "Remarks on Presenting the Presidential Medal of
    Freedom."

"A devoted family man . . .": Walton, *Made in America*, 331.

EPILOGUE

"Wal-Mart has literally . . .": Fishman, *The Wal-Mart Effect*, 229.

"There's always a challenger . . .": Walton, *Made in America*, 260.

Our Money, 2008: U.S. Bureau of Labor Statistics Consumer Expenditure
    Survey.

BIBLIOGRAPHY

"Announcing Our Remodeling Sale." Walton's 5 & 10 advertisement in the *Benton County Democrat*, July 27, 1950.

Associated Press. "Walton: Loses Another $1 Billion-Plus in Monday's Market Plunge." Oct. 19, 1987.

Barrier, Michael. "Walton's Mountain." *Nation's Business*, April 1988, 18–26.

"Battle of the Discounters." *Time*, Sept. 15, 1961.

Bender, Marylin. "Growth and Variety of Discount Houses Challenge Shopper and Store Alike." *New York Times*, Jan. 30, 1962.

"Big Business Deal Is Closed Here: Improvement in Business District Is Planned," *Benton County Democrat*, May 11, 1950, 1.

Bloch, Jeff, Christine Donahue, and Peter Newcomb. "The 400 Richest People in America." *Forbes*, Oct. 28, 1985, 108-14.

Blumenthal, Karen. "Arrival of Discounter Tears the Civic Fabric of Small-Town Life." *Wall Street Journal*, April 14, 1987, A1.

Blumenthal, Karen. "Marketing with Emotion: Wal-Mart Shows the Way." *Wall Street Journal*, Nov. 13, 1989.

Blumenthal, Karen. "Wal-Mart Founder, Walton, Undergoes Cancer Treatment." *Wall Street Journal*, Jan. 19, 1990, B5.

Bush, George. "Remarks on Presenting the Presidential Medal of Freedom to Samuel M. Walton in Bentonville, Arkansas, March 17, 1992," American Reference Library database.

Carruth, Eleanore. "Kmart Has to Open Some New Doors on the Future." *Fortune*, July 1977, 144–54.

"Cart History," www.unarco.com

Castro, Janice, with William McWhirter and Richard Woodbury. "Mr. Sam Stuns Goliath." *Time*, Feb. 25, 1991.

Cooper, Nancy. "For Richer and Richer." *Ladies' Home Journal*, May 1989, 247–48.

Current Population Reports, March 2, 1948, Bureau of the Census, U.S. Department of Commerce, Family & Individual Money Income in the US: 1945. Accessed via www.census.gov.

"Discount Houses Are Here to Stay." *BusinessWeek*, April 29, 1961, 112–15.

Dolfman, Michael L., and Denis M. McSweeney. "100 Years of U.S. Consumer Spending: Data for the Nation, New York City, and Boston." U.S. Bureau of Labor Statistics, May 2006.

Duty, James. "Hinted Racial Trouble Absent as Negro Gives Show in Rogers." *Rogers Daily News*, Jan. 25, 1962.

Ely, Kristy. "Associate Spotlight: 'One of the Good Ones'—Miss Jackie Recalls the Early Days." *Wal-Mart World*, May 1990, 5.

English, Larry. Author interview, June 23, 2010.

Fishman, Charles. *The Wal-Mart Effect: How the World's Most Powerful Company Really Works—and How It's Transforming the American Economy*. New York: Penguin Books, 2006.

Flagler Productions. Helen Walton Memorial Video.

Flagler Productions. Transcript of manager's meeting, Feb. 18, 1986.

Flagler Productions. Video of visit to Old High Middle School, mid-1980s.

"From Our Founders . . ." Interview for Wal-Mart's 25th anniversary. *Wal-Mart World*, Oct. 1987, 2–4,18. Reprinted as "Sam, Helen & Bud," *Benton County Daily Democrat*, Oct. 25, 1987, 1D.

Garcia, Guy D. "People." *Time*, March 26, 1984.

"Gibson's L'il Ole Billion-Dollar Business." *BusinessWeek*, March 20, 1971, 60–62.

Gilliam, Maggie. Author interview, June 23, 2009.

Gilman, Hank, and Karen Blumenthal. "Two Wal-Mart Officials Vie for Top Post." *Wall Street Journal*, July 23, 1986.

"Grand Opening Thursday of Walton's Re-built, Re-stocked, and Expanded Variety Store; N.W. Arkansas' Finest." *Benton County Democrat*. March 15, 1951, 1.

Greenhouse, Steven. "Workers Assail Night Lock-Ins by Wal-Mart." *New York Times*, Jan. 18, 2004.

Halverson, Richard C., "Wal-Mart: Retailer of the Decade: Generosity on a Budget." *Discount Store News*, Dec. 18, 1989.

Harris, Art. "America's Richest Man Lives . . . Here?" *Washington Post*, Nov. 17, 1985.

Harris, Monte. Author interview, June 18, 2009.

Heinbockel, C. S. "Moving up to Riches, Then Out, the Wal-Mart Way." *Arkansas Gazette,* Aug. 24, 1986, 1D.

Helliker, Kevin. "Closing the Books: Sam Walton, the Man Who Made Wal-Mart No. 1 Retailer, Dies." *Wall Street Journal,* April 6, 1992.

Hickman High School *Cresset,* 1936, accessed at www.kewpie.net/cressets.html.

"High Profile: Helen Alice Robson Walton." *Arkansas Democrat,* April 29, 1990, High Profile section, 1.

"How Kresge Became the Top Discounter." *BusinessWeek,* Oct. 24, 1970, 62–64.

"How We Promote for Higher Gross." *The Discount Merchandiser,* Aug. 1975, 60.

Huey, John. "America's Most Successful Merchant." *Fortune,* Sept. 23, 1991.

Huey, John. Author interview, Sept. 8, 2009.

Huey, John. "The Secret Life of Sam Walton." *Southpoint,* Feb. 1990, 60.

Huey, John. "Wal-Mart: Will It Take Over the World?" *Fortune,* Jan. 30, 1989.

"Hustler Walton." Beta Theta Pi fraternity article, 1940, on display at the Wal-Mart Visitors Center.

"Keeping Up with Kresge." *BusinessWeek,* Oct. 19, 1974, 70–78.

Kilborn, Peter T. "Wal-Mart's 'Buy American.'" *New York Times,* April 10, 1985.

"Kresge's Triple-Threat Retailing." *BusinessWeek,* Jan. 25, 1966, 126–34.

Leach, William. *Land of Desire: Merchants, Power, and the Rise of a New American Culture.* New York: Vintage Books, 1993.

Leveritt, Mara. "The Wal-Mart Way." *Arkansas Times,* Feb. 1984, 54–57, 105–16.

Loeb, Walter. Author interview, July 30, 2009.

Loveless, Ron. Author interview, June 19, 2009.

Mahoney, Tom, and Leonard Sloane. *Great Merchants: America's Foremost Retail Institutions and the People Who Made Them Great.* New York: Harper & Row, Publishers, 1966.

"Making the Difference: The Story of Wal-Mart." Wal-Mart Visitors Center, Bentonville, Ark., 1990.

Mason, Todd, with Marc Frons. "Sam Walton of Wal-Mart: Just Your Basic Homespun Billionaire." *BusinessWeek,* Oct. 14, 1985, 142.

McCord, Robert. "Stockholders on a Locker-Room High." *Arkansas Democrat-Gazette,* June 8, 1986.

McFadden, Robert D. "America's New Super-Rich Men: Fortunes Founded on the Prosaic." *New York Times,* Aug. 27, 1973

McManus, Kevin. "Sam's Song." *Forbes,* Jan. 4, 1982, 226.

"Miss Helen Alice Robson Weds Lieut. Samuel Moore Walton," *Tulsa Daily World*, Monday, Feb. 15, 1943.

"New Rogers Store Sets Opening." *Rogers Daily News*, June 30, 1962, 1.

Ortega, Bob. *In Sam We Trust: The Untold Story of Sam Walton and How Wal-Mart Is Devouring America.* New York: Times Business, 1998.

Pay Day, Penney company newsletter, Sept. 1941. J. C. Penney papers, DeGolyer Library, Southern Methodist University.

Penney, J. C. *Fifty Years with the Golden Rule.* New York: Harper & Brothers, Publishers, 1950.

Plunkett-Powell, Karen. *Remembering Woolworth's: A Nostalgic History of the World's Most Famous Five-and-Dime.* New York: St. Martin's Press, 1999.

Reddish, Jeannette M. "People of the Financial World." *Financial World*, Aug. 15, 1976, 28–29.

Reinboth, Gary and Lois. Author interview, June 18, 2009.

"Retailing's Great Race." *Forbes,* Nov. 15, 1968, 79.

Reuters. "'Just a Regular Guy' Puts Tiny Arkansas Town on the Map," Dec. 15, 1985.

Savitar. University of Missouri, Columbia, yearbook, 1940. Accessed at digital.library.umsystem.edu.

Schuster, Linda. "Wal-Mart Chief's Enthusiastic Approach Infects Employees, Keeps Retailer Growing." *Wall Street Journal*, April 20, 1981, 21.

Seneker, Harold. "A Day in the Life of Sam Walton." *Forbes,* Dec. 1, 1977, 45–48.

Seneker, Harold, with Jonathan Greenberg and John Dorfman. "The Forbes Four Hundred." *Forbes*, Sept. 13, 1982, 100-105.

Seneker, Harold, with Dolores Lataniotis. "The Richest People in America." *Forbes*, Oct. 21, 1991, 145-51; Oct. 19, 1992, 91-93.

Serwer, Andy, and Kate Bonamici. "The Waltons: Inside America's Richest Family." *Fortune*, Nov. 15, 2004, 42–62.

"Small-Town Hit." *Time,* May 23, 1983.

Soderquist, Don. Author interview, Aug. 6, 2009.

Soderquist, Don. *The Wal-Mart Way: The Inside Story of the Success of the World's Largest Company.* Nashville: Thomas Nelson, Inc., 2005.

"Story of a Revolution Under Way in Retailing," *U.S. News & World Report*, Sept. 25, 1961, 101–105.

Tedlow, Richard S. *New and Improved: The Story of Mass Marketing in America*. New York: Basic Books, 1990.

Tomsho, Robert. "Wal-Mart's Walton Predicts Company Could Quintuple Sales by the Year 2000." *Wall Street Journal*, June 4, 1990, B9C.

Trimble, Vance H. *Sam Walton: The Inside Story of America's Richest Man*. New York: Dutton, 1990.

"The True Look of the Discount Industry." *The Discount Merchandiser*, an annual summary of the industry, typically in the May issue, 1974–1980.

"2,000 Gather at Wal-Mart Meeting to Review 'Record-Breaking Year.'" *Arkansas Gazette*, June 7, 1986, 13A.

Walden, George. "So Long Sam: Sam Walton Became Working-Class Hero, Retailing Billionaire." *Arkansas Business*, April 13, 1992.

"Wal-Mart: A Discounter Sinks Deep Roots in Small Town, U.S.A." *BusinessWeek*, Nov. 5, 1979, 145–46.

"Wal-Mart Chief Rewards Staff with a Hula Dance." *Wall Street Journal*, March 16, 1984.

"Wal-Mart Stores Chief Resigns, Is Succeeded by Company's Founder." *Wall Street Journal*, June 29, 1976, 15.

Wal-Mart Stores, Inc. Annual reports for 1972 to 2010. Accessible at walmartstores.com, "Investors" tab, Annual reports.

Wal-Mart Stores, Inc. "Global Sustainability Report: 2010 Progress Update. Accessible at walmartstores.com, "Sustainability" tab.

Wal-Mart Stores, Inc. Prospectus for stock offering, Oct. 1, 1970

Wal-Mart Stores, Inc. Accessible at walmartstores.com, "About Us," tab, History and Culture sections.

Walton, Helen. "Season's Greetings" Christmas letter, Dec. 15, 1962. On display at the Wal-Mart Visitors Center.

Walton, Sam. "Message to Associates." *Wal-Mart World*, February/March, 1990, 3.

Walton, Sam. "Message to Associates: Our Focus for '92." *Wal-Mart World*, February 1992, 2.

Walton, Sam, with John Huey. *Sam Walton: Made in America*. New York: Bantam Books, 1992.

Walton Family Foundation, Form 990, for years 2007, 2008, 2009.

"Walton Soon to Complete Remodeling of His Variety Store Building." *Benton County Democrat,* March 5, 1951, 1.

Zimmerman, Ann. "Judge Certifies Wal-Mart as Class Action; Up to 1.6 Million Could Join Sex-Discrimination Case." *Wall Street Journal,* June 23, 2004, A1.

ACKNOWLEDGMENTS

There's a common expression among the people who run stores: Retail is detail. So, in many ways, are books, and this book wouldn't have come together without lots of detailed help from many people.

I am indebted first to those who provided crucial details to help tell Sam's story: Larry English, Maggie Gilliam, Monte Harris, John Huey, Walter Loeb, Ron Loveless, Gary and Lois Reinboth, and Don Soderquist. Others assisted with important research details: Jay Allen, John Brock at Ben Franklin, the Dallas Public Library's Interlibrary Loan, Ken Duvall, Jeff Fiedler, Joan Gosnell at Southern Methodist University, Brian Kelly at the University of Arkansas, Nelson Lichtenstein, Kent Marts, and Richard Willis.

Mary Lyn Villanueva and Gregory Pierce of Flagler Productions in Kansas City, Missouri, were beyond generous in providing assistance with their archives, helping with both facts and photographs, and Jenny McCartney provided valuable research assistance there. Additional photo help came from Marie Demeroukas of the Shiloh Museum of Ozark History, Charley Blackmore of www.kewpie.net, and Ginger Murphy of the Chisholm Trail Museum. Stuart Karle provided much needed (and detailed) advice.

My awesome agent, Ken Wright, was incredibly supportive, even when I waffled on whether Walton was a worthy subject.

At Viking, my editor, the delightful and insightful Catherine Frank, helped make this a much better book. The detail-oriented Janet Pascal kept me honest, and Jim Hoover and Kate Renner put together an energetic design that truly brings the story to life. Paul Szep, the Pulitzer Prize-winning cartoonist, responded to a query about his editorial cartoons and graciously offered to provide an illustration, which turned into an all-time favorite cover.

My many years covering Wal-Mart and overseeing the company's coverage in the *Wall Street Journal* provided the foundation for this project, and I was fortunate to travel that road with many smart and dedicated journalists, including Hank Gilman, Bob Ortega, Louise Lee, and especially Ann Zimmerman, Kevin Helliker, and Emily Nelson.

Last, there are never enough thanks for Scott, Abby and Jenny, my wonderful, patient, and supportive family.

INDEX

Numbers in *italic* refer to captions. Numbers followed by "b" refer to boxed text.

Karen Blumenthal

Mr. Sam